THE DECLINE
OF U.S.
RELIGIOUS FAITH
1912–1984
and
The Effects of Education
and Intelligence
on Such Faith

by
Burnham P. Beckwith, Ph.D.

Published by B. P. Beckwith
656 Lytton Ave. (C430), Palo Alto, CA 94301
Price: —$9.00, postpaid

This book consists largely of three separate but related essays: (1) "The Decline of U.S. Religious Faith, 1912-84," (2) "The Effect of Formal Education on U.S. Religious Faith," and (3) "The Effect of Intelligence on U.S. Religious Faith." They are closely related because the long decline of faith was largely due to the growth of both formal education and the influence of the most intelligent people. Moreover, many of the scientific studies used here to prove that religious faith has declined also contain evidence as to the effect of formal education and/or native intelligence on U.S. religious faith.

All three essays are entirely based on scientific polls of religious opinion among students and adults. Each is a review of the findings of such polls, not a review of old or new arguments or personal opinions concerning religious trends and/or their causes.

Earlier or summary versions of all three essays have been published as journal articles (Beckwith, 1980, 1981, 1985). After writing the first two of these journal articles, which were based on a very incomplete review of the literature, I began in 1981 a thorough search of the literature available in the Stanford University Libraries. As a result, the essays in this book cover many more sources and are much longer than the earlier articles. The greatest expansion is that in my essay on the decline of U.S. religious faith, which now covers over three times as many sources as the corresponding journal article. Nearly all of the additional studies reviewed here further support the main conclusions stated in my earlier articles. But I made every reasonable effort to find and review studies with contrary conclusions.

The two chief American pioneers in the use of scientific, quantitative study of American religious faith were Edwin Diller Starbuck, long-time professor of psychology at the University of Iowa, under whom I studied at the University of Southern California in 1930, and James Leuba of Bryn Mawr College.

In the preface to his book, The Psychology of Religion (1899), William James reported that he had been very skeptical when "many years ago Dr. Starbuck,

then a student at Harvard University, tried to enlist
my sympathies in his statistical inquiry into religious ideas and experiences..." By 1899, James had
modified his attitude, and highly praised Starbuck.
"He has broken ground in a new place, his only pre-
decesor...being Dr. Leuba, in his similar but less
elaborate investigation..." (Rankin, 1938: 8).

Unfortunately, Starbuck, who used questionnaires
to study the conversion process, failed to go on and
use them to study trends in religious faith, much
more important phenomena. In the latter field, Leuba
was the brilliant pioneer.

In addition to providing the above historical
information, Fay S. Rankin has reported that "Leuba,
in his doctoral dissertation published in 1896, made
a plea for application of the scientific method to
the study of religion....not only did he point out
the need for scientific data...he also presented the
results of an investigation of religious experiences
which he made through the use of a questionnaire....
By 1912 he had written 23 papers relating to religious life" (ibid: 9).

To save space and to simplify my discussion, I
have deliberately refrained from detailed criticism
of the statistical methods used in the studies
reviewed. All of these methods were imperfect, but
nearly all included such essentials of scientific
polling as random selection of subjects and were chosen and used by reasonably competent researchers.

When I first conceived of the idea of writing a
book on the decline of religion, I went to the
central catalog of the nearby 5-million-volume
Stanford University Library System to find out how
many books had already been published on this extremely significant intellectual and historical trend.
To my astonishment, I could find not a single book or
journal article with the title, "the decline of
religion" or any synonymous title. I kept looking for
such a book throughout the next two years but never
found one.

In my search I checked a score of modern history
books for references to such a book or article, but
could find none. Moreover, as explained in detail
later (pp. 3-5), I found that these history books had
little if anything to say about the decline of
religion.

One reason why the authors of textbooks on
modern U.S. history have had little if anything to say
about the long decline of religious faith is that
they have lacked a comprehensive summary of the

evidence for this decline since 1912. The chief purpose of this monograph is to provide such a summary.

A history of the past is most useful and relevant when it enables us to predict the future. I believe that my history of the decline of U.S. religious faith, and the related essays, justify relatively firm and important predictions concerning the future trend in U.S. religious faith. The last chapter in this book is devoted to such predictions.

CONTENTS

PREFACE iii

I. THE DECLINE OF U.S. RELIGIOUS FAITH,
    1912-84   1
    A. Historians' Reports of U.S.
        Religious Trends   3
    B. The Decline of U.S. Student Faith .   5
    C. The Decline of U.S. Lay Adult
        Faith 22
    D. The Decline of Faith Among U.S.
        Clergymen 31
    E. General Conclusions on Decline
        in U.S. Faith   34
    F. Contrary Views — Caplow et al,
        1983   37
    G. Church Membership and Attendance
        Trends   38
    H. Reasons for the Decline in Faith . . 40

II. THE EFFECT OF EDUCATION ON U.S.
    RELIGIOUS FAITH 41
    A. The Effect of Education on U.S.
        Student Faith 42
    B. Studies of College Professors . . . 65
    C. The Effect of Education on U.S.
        Adult Faith   70
    D. Aging and Religious Faith 77
    E. Sex and Religious Faith 77
    F. Race and Religious Faith 78
    G. General Conclusions 78
    H. Explanation 79

III. THE EFFECT OF INTELLIGENCE ON U.S.
     RELIGIOUS FAITH 82
    A. Individual Student Intelligence
        and Religious Faith 84
    B. Student-Body Comparisons 95
    C. The Religious Faith of College
        Professors 99
    D. Studies of Very-High-IQ Groups . . . 99
    E. Studies of Success and Religiosity . 101
    F. Gallup Public Opinion Polls 105
    G. Studies of College Classes   105
    H. Aging and Religious Faith 105
    I. Conclusions 106
    J. Explanation 107

IV. THE FUTURE OF U.S. RELIGIOUS FAITH   109
     A. The Reasons Why U.S. Religious
        Faith Will Decline   109
     B. A Comment on Wuthnow's
        Criticism   113
     C. Group Differences in Religious
        Faith   113
     D. Why Americans Are More Religious
        than Europeans   116
     E. The Future Overall Trend in U.S.
        Religious Faith   118
     F. Lenski's Bad Prediction   118
     G. The Rate of Future Decline
        in U.S. Faith   119
     H. Predictions on Group Religious
        Faith Trends   121
     I. Predictions on Belief in Individual
        Dogmas   123
     J. Future Research Trends   124

POSTSCRIPT   127

REFERENCES   129

INDEX OF NAMES   141

ABOUT THE AUTHOR   144

CHAPTER I

THE DECLINE OF U.S. RELIGIOUS FAITH, 1912-84

Religious faith, i.e., belief in religious doctrines, has played an extraordinary role in human
history since the dawn of civilization, and long
before. It has not only determined all religious
behavior, a major part of human life, but has
strongly influenced nearly all other human activities. Therefore, the decline of religious faith in
the West since the Renaisance is one of the most
important, perhaps the most important, of all
historical trends since 1500. It is remarkable that
no book devoted to the scientific evidence of this
trend has ever been published.
     Since this is a study of religious faith in a
predominantly Christian country, the United States,
the religious faith studied is largely Christian
faith, but it includes some dogmas accepted also by
Jews and Moslems. As used here, the term religious
faith denotes belief in basic Christian dogmas,
including belief in a personal humanoid God who
observes human conduct, answers prayers, and rewards
or punishes human beings in this world and/or in an
imagined other world. Such religious faith declines
both when believers become less firm in their belief
and/or when they cease to believe in one or more
basic religious dogmas.
     Belief in religious dogmas may vary indepen-
dantly of religious behavior or attitudes towards
religion or the church. Thus church attendance may
rise, and attitudes toward religion may improve, in
spite of, or because of, the rejection by religious
people of old religious dogmas such as those concerning hell and creationism.
     This chapter is a survey and critical review of
nearly all published quantitative scientific evidence
concerning the decline of religious faith in the U.S.
Little such evidence was available before 1910, but
the amount of it has been steadily increasing since
then, and the great majority of it supports the
conclusion that there has been a radical and almost
continuous decline in religious faith since 1912.
So far as I am aware, this essay is the first review
of this literature.

-1-

Although I am primarily concerned with the trend in U.S. religious faith, not trends in U.S. religious behavior, I shall occasionally use data on trends in such behavior when it is persuasive evidence of a similar trend in belief.

It is remarkable that nearly all of the serious investigations into religious opinion and changes in religious belief have been financed and carried out by secular agencies. One would reasonably assume that the clergy is more interested in the effect of their teaching upon religious faith than any secular agencies, but they have displayed a notable disinterest in such investigations. They have not even compiled reliable data on church membership and attendance, and have almost completely neglected the scientific study of changes in religious faith, perhaps for the fear of what they might discover.

A great many writers have expressed their personal opinion concerning the rise or fall of religious faith in America, but the vast majority have failed to offer any statistics on public opinion to support their opinion. In this essay I make no effort to review such expressions of personal opinion. I am here concerned only with quantitative evidence which might be used to support or disprove such opinions.

In 1958 Michael Argyle, an Oxford University psychologist, published an excellent book, Religious Behavior, which summarized scientifie evidence on recent trends in such behavior in both the U.K. and the U.S. It contains several pages of incidental remarks on religious belief (few of which are listed under "belief" in the Subject Index). In 1975 he co-authored The Social Psychology of Religion, but this contains little more data on trends in religious faith.

The most complete review of the quantitative evidence of the decline of U.S. religious faith is that in Dean Hoge's book, Commitment on Campus (1974), but it reviews only the trend in religious faith among U.S. college students. In this essay I not only cover in more detail the evidence he cites, but also review much additional evidence on student trends, and nearly all available evidence on the trend in religious belief among U.S. adults.

This chapter consists largely of two main sections, a review of all the religious polls which reveal the trend in religious faith among students and a review of all the religious polls which reveal the trend in such faith among U.S. adults. Before I begin my review of student polls, I wish to review briefly the treatment of the long decline of U.S. religious faith by authors of books on recent or modern U.S. history.

A. Historians' Reports on U.S. Religious Trends

I have reviewed the indexes and tables of contents of more than a score of general histories of the U.S., searching for reports of the rise or fall of religious faith and behavior in America since 1865, and have been surprised to discover how little historians record about these subjects. Some long indexes do not even list the subject religion, and others give only one or two page references. The most complete record I could find was that in volume II of The Growth of the American Republic (1980) written by S. E. Morison, H. S. Commager, and W. E. Leuchtenberg. The term religion is listed in the index, with 13 page citations. But only 6 of these references deal with religious faith, and then primarily and very briefly, with the effect of "the higher criticism" and Darwinian theory on faith. According to the authors, these two factors "paved the way for the rejection of much [dogma] ...and for a liberal religion..." Darwinism was given a religious interpretation and was increasingly accepted by "distinguished clergymen" (p. 201). However, the authors offered no statistical or other evidence for these claims, which they did not elaborate.

In their two-volume History of the American People (1958) Harry J. Carman and Harold C. Syrett discussed very briefly the effect of Darwin's theory of evolution and of higher criticism of the Bible on American religious faith, and reported that, "Despite the vehemence with which they defended their position, the upholders of the orthodox view were generally compelled to retreat as an increasing number of Americans...came to view Holy Writ less as an infallible record of a past era and more as a moral guide and literary masterpiece" (II, 219). This was their most complete report of the decline of religious faith in the 19th century. They cited no evidence for their assertion that such a decline had occurred.

Dexter Perkins and G. G. Van Deusen are the authors of a two-volume book, The United States of America, A History (1968). Volume II (since 1965)

-3-

does not even list the term religion in its index.
Nor does it list abortion or birth control. It does
list Darwin, with three page references, but it does
not report a long-run decline of religious faith.
    Franklin L. Baumer, the author of Religion and
the Rise of Scepticism (1960) and Modern European
Thought (1977), quoted with approval Dietrich Bonhoeffer's assertion that the secularization movement,
which Bonhoeffer believed had begun in the 13th century, "has in our time reached a certain completion.
Man has learned to cope with all questions of importance without recourse to God..." (Baumer, 1977: 439-
40). Bonhoeffer was probably correct as to the 600-
year decline of religion in Europe, but he cited no
evidence, and his claim that this decline had reached some kind of "completion" is certainly far from
true.
    Baumer also quoted the 1946 claim by the philo-
sopher Emmanuel Mounier that, "Where a century ago,
among a hundred men, you could count a majority pro-
fessing Christian doctrines...nowadays you would
doubtless find some 10% of Christian believers..."
Baumer commented that, "Professor Mounier's statistics may not be exact, but statements such as his...
are legion..." (Baumer, 1960: 226). In fact, there
were no such statistics in 1946. The claims of historians concerning the decline of religions are apparently based upon literary research and personal
experiences, not upon statistics of any kind.
    Although nearly all the historians who have
discussed past religious trends in the U.S. and Europe have reported a long decline in religious faith,
none of them have offered or referred to scientific
studies as evidence of such a decline. In fact, few
if any such studies were available before Leuba began
his research. However, the number of studies since
he pioneered the way has increased greatly, and al-
together they offer convincing proof of a long decline in religious faith. I hope that historians
will soon begin to cite such studies as evidence for
their conclusions on U.S. religious trends since
1900.
    While there is little if any quantitative data
concerning the decline of U.S. religious faith during the 19th century, there is a great deal of such
data concerning the growth of secondary and higher
education during this period. If each year of additional secondary and higher education made U.S.
adults less religious during the 20th century, as
demonstrated in Chapter II, it is highly likely that

it had a similar effect during the previous century, and, therefore, that there was an almost steady decline in religious faith during the 19th century.

Why have American historians had so little to say about this major historical trend? I believe they feared that their histories would be excluded from many U.S. schools and libraries if they offered an adequate account of the decline of U.S. religious faith. The same reason has persuaded most authors of textbooks on biology to minimize their discussion of the theory of evolution, or to ignore this theory completely.

B. The Decline of U.S. Student Faith

The first reliable quantitative evidence concerning the decline of religious faith in advanced countries was provided by American college professors of psychology and sociology who, in the first decades of this century, began to question their students concerning their religious faith. They were familiar with the new statistical techniques required to obtain reliable results from opinion polls, and they produced many very significant studies.

1. Leuba's Pioneer Studies, 1912-33

James H. Leuba (1868-1946), long-time professor of psychology at Bryn Mawr College, was the first person to use religious questionnaires to determine scientifically the trend in U.S. religious faith. In 1912 and 1914 he used questionnaires to investigate the degree of belief in a personal God and in personal immortality among three classes of people: (1) college students, (2) scientists listed in Cattell's American Men of Science (1910), and (3) members of the American Sociological Society and of the American Psychological Association. In 1933 he again used the same questions to determine the religious beliefs of the same three classes of people. By comparing the 1912-14 data with the 1933 data, he proved scientifically, for the first time, that there had been a significant decline in religious faith.

Leuba claimed that "the rules governing scientific statistics have been followed" in his research (Leuba, 1950: 19). He used objective standards to select a sufficiently large number of subjects, and obtained useful answers from over 80% of those queried.

In this section I shall review only his study of the trend in student religious faith.

In 1912 he submitted four questions on religious faith, including one on belief in a personal God, to the students of a number of classes in nine highranking and one average school, including some women's colleges. He found that 56% of the men and 83% of the women declared a belief in a personal God who answers prayers.

In 1933 he queried all the students in college A, ("high-ranking") and college B, ("definitely radical") on belief in such a personal God. He secured answers from 90% and 93% of the students. In college A, only 31% of the replies reported belief in a personal God; in college B, only 11% did so.

These data suggest a rate of decline in belief in a fundamental religious dogma so rapid as to be incredible, a rate probably due largely to marked differences in the student groups compared. As later studies revealed, religious belief is much lower in high-ranking than in low-ranking schools.

Leuba also queried all students in college A (Bryn Mawr) on their belief in immortality in both 1914 and 1933. He found that about 72% reported such belief in 1914, and only about 39% in 1933 (ibid: 49). The proportion of disbelievers grew from about 6% to about 24%. Although these data are for the same college, there must have been major changes in the student groups queried, because the rate of decline still seems almost incredible.

2. Hoge's Replication of Leuba's Polls

Leuba was the brilliant pioneer who first used scientific opinion polls to demonstrate a long-run decline in religious faith and a significant correlation between rejection of religion and amount of education and/or intelligence in the U.S. The next most productive researcher on U.S. student religious trends was Dean R. Hoge, professor of sociology at the Princeton Theological Seminary. He wrote his Harvard Ph.D. thesis on his research on these trends, and later published his data in Commitment on Campus (1974) and in several journal articles. He searched out and replicated nearly all relevant earlier student polls. The results provided a convincing confirmation of Leuba's conclusion that student religious faith was declining. He did not try to verify Leuba's more striking conclusion that religious faith varies inversely with education and intelligence.

In 1968 Hoge replicated Leuba's poll on belief in a personal God at college A, which he identified

as Bryn Mawr. He asked the same question in the
same college, and reported that the percent of believers in a personal God had declined from 31% in
1933 to 19% in 1968 (Hoge, 1974: 48). He could not
replicate the similar 1912 polls in the other schools
because he could not find out which schools had been
covered. Unfortunately, he also failed to replicate
Leuba's brilliant pioneer study of the trend in
religious belief among scientists.

In 1968 Hoge also replicated Leuba's 1933 poll
on belief in immortality at college A, and reported
that belief had declined further, from 39% in 1933
to 24% in 1968. He adjusted the former figure to
45% and the latter to 33%—to allow for changes in
the types of subjects—which reduced the rate of
decline, but left it still rapid. The overall un-
adjusted decline from 72% in 1914 to 24% in 1968 was
even more rapid (ibid: 47).

3. The Lynd-Caplow Middletown Surveys, 1924-78

In 1924-25 Robert and Helen Lynd made a study of
a midwestern community they called Middletown. As
part of their study, they gave some 1200 high school
students an attitude test which included six questions on religion. In 1977, sociologists Theodore
Caplow and Howard M. Bahr replicated this test on all
Middletown High School students. They found a radical decrease in religiosity on all six religious
issues.

For instance, they learned that belief in the
theory of evolution had grown from 28% to 50%, that
belief that Christ was "entirely perfect" had fallen
from 83% to 68%, that belief in the Bible as "a
sufficient guide to all problems" had fallen from
74% to 50%, and that belief that it was wrong to go
to the movies on Sunday had fallen from 33% to 6%
(Caplow and Bahr, 1979: 5).

4. The Katz-Allport-Hoge Syracuse Polls, 1926-68

In 1926 Daniel Katz and Floyd Allport polled
some 1500 Syracuse University liberal arts students,
asking seven questions concerning their belief in a
deity. The first question asked about belief in a
personal creator who answers prayers; and the second,
about belief in an intelligent friendly being and in
prayer as communion with nature. Some 26% of the
freshmen and 15% of the seniors checked the first
belief, and 44% and 46% the second belief (Katz and
Allport, 1931: 268).

By combining the figures for answers to these two questions, Katz and Allport achieved figures on belief in God which approximated Leuba's 1914 figures for belief in a personal God who answers prayers. They concluded that "the incidence of belief in a personal deity appears to have changed but little from 1914 to 1926 (Katz and Allport, 1931: 390). But Leuba later claimed that only the answers to the first question were comparable with his data, and asserted that they confirmed his 1933 findings, which had recorded a drastic decline in student religious faith (Leuba, 1950: 27-28). I agree with Leuba.

In 1968 Hoge replicated the Katz-Allport Syracuse study. He did not report separately on answers to each of the first two questions. Instead, he combined the answers, and reported that "the adjusted responses showed a decline of 14 percentage points in the two most orthodox response categories..." He also reported that the changes from 1926 to 1968 in belief in "the miracles of the Bible...were minimal" (Hoge, 1974; 46-47).

5.   The Dudycha-Hoge Ripon Data, 1929-68

In 1950 George J. Dudycha published a scientific comparison of the reported religious beliefs of 266 Ripon freshmen he had tested in 1929 with the reported beliefs of 852 Ripon freshmen who took the same test in 1949. The test consisted of 25 major Christian doctrines, for which students were allowed five degrees of acceptance, ranging from "implicitly believe" to "absolutely do not believe." Dudycha reported that, "On the whole, the extent to which college freshmen believe various fundamental religious beliefs is about the same in 1949 as it was...in 1930," the coefficient of correlation being .95. However, there were four doctrines for which a statistically significant change occurred, and in all four cases the change was towards less belief. Dudycha therefore reported that, "The chief difference...is that the 1949 freshmen show a slight tendency toward somewhat less belief in some of the religious propositions than the 1930 freshmen did" (Dudycha, 1959: 166-8).

In 1968 Hoge replicated the Dudycha test at Ripon College. He reported that, "From 1929 to 1949 the average change on 23 items for those who 'absolutely believe' or 'are inclined to believe but doubt' was a decline of about 2 percentage points....

From 1949 to 1968 the average change was a decline
of 17.6 percentage points." When these figures
were adjusted for changes in the groups tested, the
2 point decline became a 3.7 point rise, and the
17.6 point decline became a 14.3 point decline,
yielding a net adjusted decline of 10.6 points from
1929 to 1968 (Hoge, 1974: 44).

6. The Sheldon-Hoge Wisconsin Studies, 1931-68

    In the years 1928-31 William H. Sheldon admini-
stered a "Wisconsin Scale of Radicalism and Conservatism" to many of his Wisconsin psychology classes,
and to some sociology classes, and 3,010 responses
were received. His poll included queries on four
religious beliefs: the reality of divine inspiration, the supernatural idea, individual immortality,
and the idea of God.
    In 1968 Hoge repeated the Sheldon Wisconsin
polls and reported "small gains in belief in divine
inspiration, the importance of belief in God, and
individual immortality." He noted that such a
"shift toward orthodoxy...was not found in any
other college in our research." As a partial explanation of this anomaly, he added that "Wisconsin
was known as a liberal college in the 1920's and
1930's (Hoge, 1974: 45).
    However, the data given in Appendix B reveal
that denial of divine inspiration rose from 27 to
35%, that belief that religion should deal with
the supernatural fell from 44 to 37%, and that the
percent of those who believed that there is probably or definitely no such thing as divine inspiration rose from 27 to 35%. Only belief in individual
immortality increased much, from 34 to 44%. Belief
in a personal God declined slightly, from 35 to 33%
(ibid: 202-03). Moreover, approval of birth control
increased radically. Therefore, I conclude that
this study did not reveal the "shift toward orthodoxy" reported by Hoge. Rather, it revealed a small
but significant decline in religious faith.

7. The V. Jones Clark University Study, 1931-67

    In the years 1931-35, 1947-49, 1954-56, and
1967 Vernon Jones of Clark University gave the
Thurstone-Chave Attitude Toward the Reality of God
test to all entering freshmen at his school. The
minimum score on this test was zero (atheism), and
the maximum was 11. He reported   that the mean

-9-

score for 286 men in the years 1930-33 was 7.23
(SD 1.52) while the mean score for 190 men in 1967
was 6.28 (SD 1.78). He also noted that freshmen
belief declined much faster than senior belief
(V. Jones, 1970: 37).

In a 1974 review of these findings, Hoge adjusted the 1967 figure from 6.28 to 6.84 to allow
for changes in the samples, primarily an influx of
Jewish students, who are less religious than Christian students (Hoge, 1974: 43).

The Thurstone-Chave test included two questions which were most revealing as to religious
faith (3 and 20). Item #3 was, "I trust in God to
support the right and condemn the wrong." Among
Clark freshmen, belief in this statement rose from
53% in 1931 and 1934 to 61% in 1954-56 and then fell
to 41% in 1967. On the other hand, belief in item
#20, "God has no place in my thinking," rose from
5% in 1931 and 1934 to 16% in 1967 (V. Jones, 1970:
39). The small reported increase in faith from
1934 and 1931 to 1949-47 may have been largely or
entirely due to the fact that the earlier figure
was for males only, while the later figure was for
a group about 38% female.

8.   Hunter Converse-College Polls, 1934-49

During the years 1934 to 1949 all members (70-
151) of each new freshman class at Converse College,
a small southern, liberal arts, nondenominational
womens' college, were given E. C. Hunter's Social
Attitudes Test. It consisted of 94 items, including ten on religious attitudes. On the basis of
answers to these ten questions, Hunter concluded
that "A slight downward trend in liberalism toward
religion over the past 16 years can be detected from
the curve." He reported that the percentage of
students who gave liberal answers fell from about
26% in 1934-35 to about 21% in 1948-49, and the
percentage of conservatives rose from about 64% in
1934-35 to about 67% in 1948-49 (Hunter, 1951: 293).
Hunter did not state his ten religious queries,
so I do not know how many of them concerned religious faith. Trends in such faith differ from those
in religious behavior and in attitudes towards the
church and/or religion. Thus the implication of
his findings as to the trend in religious faith are
very uncertain.

9. Zelan on NORC Apostasy Data, 1933-58

In 1958 the National Opinion Research Center polled 2842 arts and science graduate students in 25 schools. The poll included questions on current religious preference and on home or parental religion, which permits determination of apostasy rates. Joseph Zelan (U.C., Berkeley sociologist) analyzed the data, and reported that 25% of the students marked "none" for religious preference, and that 50% of these "had been reared in some religion. This is a striking rate of religious apostasy" (Zelan, 1968: 371). It is noteworthy that this "striking" inter-generational change occurred largely during the period 1933-58 when some writers have claimed that there was a revival of religious faith.

Zelan also reported that "The apostasy rate among original Roman Catholics was 12%; among original Protestants, 26%; and among original Jews, 34%."

10. Hadden, 1936-61

If college students were as religious as their parents, there would be a high correlation between religiosity scores for students and those for their parents. In a 1963 report of his analysis of data from a 1961 study of 261 University of Wisconsin seniors, sociologist Jeffrey K. Hadden reported that the correlation between student religiosity and father's regular church attendance was only .27, and the like correlation for mothers was only .33 (Hadden, 1963: 212). This suggests rapid secularization in one generation, i.e., from 1936 to 1961, a generation in which a religious revival was often reported.

11. Gilliland-Hoge Polls at Northwestern, 1933-67

At Northwestern University, the Thurstone-Chave Reality of God scale (No. 22A) was give to introductory psychology classes in 1933, 1949, and several intervening years by A. R. Gilliland. He reported that the mean score for belief rose almost steadily from 6.6 in 1933 to 7.77 in 1949 (Gilliland, 1953: 114). Hoge replicated this test in 1967, and reported that the mean score had fallen to 6.26 in 1967, a little below the 1933 level (Hoge, 1974: 43). Gilliland's findings are noteworthy because they are among the very few which cover trends in student faith between 1933 and 1949, and because they support Hoge's dubious conclusion that there was a

rise in the level of U.S. student religious faith
during these years.

12.   The Allport-Hoge Harvard Polls, 1920-66

In 1946, when G.W. Allport was at Harvard, he
and two associates (J. M. Gillespie and J. Young)
queried 501 Harvard and Radcliffe students on their
religious faith. Unfortunately, they not only failed
to use Leuba's 1914-33 questions but even changed
the questions Katz and Allport had used in 1930.
Their new questionnaire offered seven alternative
positions on belief in "the Deity." They reported
that "only about one-fifth of the men and two-fifths
of the women in our study subscribe to the extreme
theistic position" [belief in a personal God], and
that 32% consider themselves atheists and agnostics
(Allport et al, 1948: 21).
In 1946 Allport et al also queried Harvard and
Radcliffe students on the relation of their religious
faith to that of their parents' faith. The replies
revealed an intergenerational decline in religious
faith, from about 1920 to 1946. For instance, 30% of
Harvard students with a religious family background
now claimed to have no need for religion (17%), or
were doubtful about such a need (13%). Although 44%
had been reared as Protestants, only 18% still chose
this faith. For Catholics, the figures were 16% and
11% respectively; for Jews 17% and 6% (ibid: 13).
The researchers concluded that, "without the
possibility of doubt," their data "reflect a genuine
trend towards secularization. The trend, of course,
is now new, but has been going on for several past
generations" (ibid: 15-16). They did not mention
Leuba's research on this subject.
In 1966 Hoge replicated the 1946 Allport study.
He found that among Harvard nonveteran students
belief in a personal God had fallen from 25% in 1946
to 16% in 1966, and then adjusted the 1966 figure
downward to about 14% "to remove the effects of
changes in religious backgrounds." The percent of
atheists grew from at least 9% to at least 20% (some
categories include both deists and atheists).
For Radcliffe students, the percent claiming
belief in a personal God fell from 40% to 13% (14%
adjusted), and the minimum percent of atheists rose
from 11 to 22% (Hoge, 1974: 36).
In addition to the seven-part question on
belief in God, the 1946 Allport poll included a
query concerning belief in immortality. When Hoge

repeated this query in 1966, the percent of those claiming to believe in immortality fell 13 percentage points below the 1946 level at Harvard; and 16 points at Radcliffe, all 1966 figures adjusted by Hoge (ibid: 38).

13. Rossman-Harvard-Crimson Study, 1935-59

In 1959 the Harvard Crimson sent an 82-item questionnaire on religious and political subjects—personal history, behavior, and opinion—to 400 Harvard and Radcliffe undergraduates, and obtained 319 returns. It found that only 23% of the respondents claimed to believe in a personal God, and that 25% claimed to be agnostics or atheists. Only 24% believed in immortality, and only 14% in Hell. The great majority (59%) had been raised as Protestants, but over 26% of these had rejected the parental faith (Rossman, 1960: 26, 28, 33). This suggests a rapid decline in religious faith in one generation (1935-59) within the kind of family who send children to Harvard.

14. The Allport-Hoge Data on L.A.C.C., 1948-67

The seven Allport questions on belief in God were also given to students at the Los Angeles City College in 1948, and later replicated by Hoge in 1967. He reported that the percent of male believers in a personal God fell from 34% in 1948 to 25% (24% adjusted) in 1967. For women, the figures were 37% and 38% (adjusted). The net overall decline was from 35.5% to 31.5%.
The smallness of the overall decline at L.A.C.C. was probably due to special factors. For instance, L.A.C.C. had minimal entrance requirements in 1967 while most of the other schools reviewed here had been raising their already high requirements during the 1948-67 period (Hoge, 1974: 35-36).

15. Heath on Haverford College Data, 1948-68

From 1948 to 1968, Haverford College gave the Minnesota Multiphase Personality Inventory Test to all entering freshmen (average number about 73) shortly after their entry. This test included questions on five basic Christian dogmas—the second coming of Christ, life hereafter, devil-hell, existence of "God," and Christ's miracles.

Douglas H. Heath, a Haverford psychologist, used the even-year answers to these five questions by about 67% of each class to prepare a "traditional belief index." He gave equal weight to each question. He reported that this belief index rose from 42% in 1948 to 47% in 1956, and then fell irregularly to a low of 31% in 1968. Belief in God fell from 79% in 1948 to 58% in 1968, and belief in "devil-hell" from 24% to 15% (Heath, 1969: 343).

Heath concluded that "The principal and most impressively consistent finding is that the religious beliefs, values, practice, and mode of thought of the freshmen of the sixties are much less orthodox than those of the youths of the late forties and fifties" (ibid: 345).

16. Wuthnow, University of California, 1945-71

In 1973 Robert Wuthnow and Charles Y. Glock published an analysis of the data on student and parental religious orientation obtained by the Institute for Social Research (Berkeley) in a 1970-71 survey of the opinions of some 2000 U.C. male freshmen and seniors. They reported that, while only 15% of the students claimed to have been raised by non-religious parents, 47% of the freshmen and 52% of the seniors classified themselves as "agnostic, atheist, or as having no religion" (Wuthnow and Glock, 1973: 161, 163). These figures imply a rapid decline in religious faith in one generation. They also imply that most loss of faith occurred in high school, not in college.

The authors reported that, "Studies of general samples of the total student population conducted in 1967 and 1971 found respectively 33% and 37% saying that they were without religion," and concluded that "religious defection is the main order of the day at Berkeley..." One reason that the 37% for 1971 is lower than the previously noted 47% and 52% for 1970-71 is that the 37% figure covers the total student population, including female and graduate students, while the higher figures cover only male freshmen and seniors. Moreover, the authors explained that "the wordings of the questions on religion in the earlier studies makes it likely that the amount of religious defection was under-estimated" (ibid: 160).

17. Hoge on University of Denver Data, 1948-68

In 1948,   622 University of Denver students
were polled on some of their religious beliefs.   In
1968 Hoge replicated this poll with 319 Denver students.   He reported that for six religious questions,
the average percent giving orthodox answers fell by
22 points.   On the question of whether the Bible "is
the inspired word of God," the "yes" answers by
"students of Protestant background" fell from 51% to
33%.   The percent of these who believed that "the
idea of God is unnecessary" rose from 6% to 17%.
Hoge concluded that "In general the changes at Denver
resemble those at Harvard, Radcliffe, and Williams"
(Hoge, 1974: 38-39).

18. The Hoge Dartmouth and Michigan Studies, 1958-68

In 1952 the Cornell Values Study questioned men
students in 11 U.S.colleges and universities on value
beliefs, including some religious beliefs.   Students
at Dartmouth (N=365) and the University of Michigan
(N=488) were queried.   In 1968 Hoge replicated the
Dartmouth survey, and, in 1969, the Michigan survey.
He reported that "belief in a Divine God, Creator of
the Universe," had fallen from 35% to 26% at Dartmouth, and from 47% to 30% at Michigan.   Moreover,
support for the next most religious alternative answer, "Belief in a power greater than myself," had
also fallen, from 30% to 26% at Dartmouth, and from
27% to 22% at Michigan (Hoge, 1971: 177).

19. The Hastings-Hoge Williams College Polls, 1948-74

In 1948 Philip K. Hastings of Williams College
surveyed some 200 Williams students, using Allport's
1946 Harvard questionnaire on religion.   The same
survey was repeated again in 1967 and 1974, and revealed a drastic decline in religious faith.   For
instance, nonveteran student belief in a personal
deity fell from 56% in 1948 to 35% in 1967, and was
still 35% in 1974.   Belief in personal immortality
fell even faster from 38% in 1948 to 17% in 1967, but
rose to 22% in 1974.   The proportion of students who
believed that "Religion and science clearly support
one another" declined from 38, to 16, to 12% (Hastings and Hoge, 1976: 242).
Apostasy rates, the percent of students who
had given up their parents' faith, rose rapidly in
both periods.   The percent for Catholics rose from

27 in 1948, to 35 in 1967, and to 70 in 1974. For
the Protestants the figures were 42, 66, and 78.
For the Jews, 22, 50, and 48. These figures suggest
a sharp decline in religious faith during both periods. According to Hastings and Hoge, the authors of
a 1976 analysis of the Williams College data, "The
overall pattern is a 'liberal shift.' A large number
of students reared as Catholics and Protestants have
shifted to liberalized Protestantism or ethical, but
not theological, Christianity, 'other' and no religious preferences at all." In 1974, 32% of all students stated their religious preference as "none"
(ibid: 241).

The Williams surveys also revealed that the percent of students who prayed "daily" or "fairly
frequently" fell from 39 in 1948, to 24 in 1967, and
to 16 in 1974 (ibid: 246), a rapidly accelerating
rate of decline.

20. Hoge's Conclusions, 1914-74

Dean Hoge not only conducted or reported more
replications of earlier surveys on U.S. student religious faith than any other researcher, thus greatly
enriching our knowledge of long-run trends in student
faith, but also published the most complete and authoritative review of the 1914-68 literature on such
trends in his book Commitment on Campus (1974). In
it he concluded that, "In summary, all studies agree
that orthodoxy declined from the late 1940's to 1966-
68.... The decline...was about 13 to 23 points...in
all colleges except L.A. City College, where the
decline was about 9 points" (Hoge, 1974: 42).
However, he also concluded that student orthodoxy probably rose substantially from 1938 to 1955,
after a long decline from 1900, or earlier, to 1938
(ibid: 52, 54-55). He claimed that "levels of orthodoxy in the middle 1920's resemble those in the
early or middle 1950's, "and that "Levels in the
middle 1930's generally resemble those in the late
1960's." However, at Bryn Mawr, the only school for
which we have trend data from 1914 to 1968, belief
in a personal God and immortality declined greatly
from 1933 to 1968, after a radical decline from
1914 to 1933.
Most of Hoge's data which suggest that student
faith grew from the 1930's to 1955 is very question-
able because it covers behavior as well as faith, or
because it is based on answers to relatively unrevealing questions concerning the reality of God,

undefined, or concerning religious preference.

Hoge's data concerning the sharp decline in student religious faith from the 1950's to 1967 is far more complete, relevant, and persuasive than his data suggesting a rise in such faith from the late 1930's to the 1950's. However, there may well have been some temporary revival of professions of such faith from 1940 to 1955 due to World War II and/or the succeeding cold war. Four of the studies reviewed in this chapter—Dudycha, Sheldon-Hoge, V. Jones, and Gilliland-Hoge—suggest that the decline in religious faith among students ceased or reversed itself during 1940-55.

According to Robert Wuthnow of Princeton University, "During the 1950's, a so-called religious revival was widely acknowledged and virtually all religious indicators, except perhaps theologically conservative belief, demonstrated growth...(my italics, Wuthnow, 1976: 837). This supports my doubt concerning Hoge's conclusion that student religious faith revived from   1935 to 1955.

21. The Young-Holtzman Texas University Polls,1955-64

A test of trends in attitudes toward the church is not as relevant to this study as a test of trends in faith in specific religious dogmas, but it has been shown that these trends were similar to belief trends among students in the years 1930-67 (V. Jones, 1970: 32, 39).

In 1955, 1958 and 1964, Wayne H. Holtzman, Robert K. Young, and associates measured the attitudes towards organized religion among 1601 undergraduate students at the University of Texas, where they taught. Their 23-item test included at least one doctrinal item, "There is no God," the responses to which were separately tabulated.

For the test as a whole, the possible score ranged "from 0, an extremely negative attitude, to 92, an extremely positive attitude." They reported a "highly significant" decline in favorable attitudes toward the church, from 63.4 in 1955 to 55.5 in 1964. And the percent of students who "strongly disagree" with the statement, "There is no God," fell from 78 in 1958 to 65 in 1964 (Young et al, 1966: 40-41).

22.   The National Review Polls, 1961-70

In both 1961-63 and 1969-70 the National Review,

William Buckley's conservative magazine, polled sophomores, juniors, and seniors in 12 widely differing American colleges and Universities on many subjects, including their religious beliefs and behavior. The polls covered different percentages of students in different schools, but, on each campus, "a sufficiently large sample...to assure statistical reliability" (NR, 1971: 635-36). The two polls were similar, not identical, but the editors did not hesitate to compare the results. Unfortunately, the National Review did not describe the inter-poll differences in the religious questions. The reported over-all figures are averages of the school averages, not averages of all students responding.

In both 1961-63 and 1969-70, students were polled on their conception of God. In the first poll, 30% reported that they believed in a God who is "omniscient, omnipotent, three-personal" and who maintains "an active concern for human affairs." In the second poll, this share had fallen to 17%. Unfortunately, the National Review failed to use the questions Leuba had used, which would have permitted more accurate determination of the long-run rate of decline in belief in a personal God, but their results clearly demonstrated an abnormally rapid decline in student religious faith from 1961 to 1969.

The National Review reported that "the sharp decline in religious orthodoxy...is especially evident in the two identifiably 'religious' schools, Marquette and Brandeis. Where 51% of the students at Brandeis expressed belief in a one person God then, 35% do now.... at Marquette...94% affirmed the divinity of Christ then, 65% do now"(ibid: 640).

According to the National Review, "All but a small fraction of the students...had been raised in some religious tradition... [but] Having reached college age, 24% said they 'wholly reject' the tradition in which they were raised...and 61% said they 'partially agree,' [but] with 'important reservations'." This suggests a marked intergenerational decline in religious faith between 1945 and 1970.

23. Caplovitz-Sherrow Apostasy Study, 1961-69

In 1961-63, the National Opinion Research Council (NORC) polled college seniors in 135 U.S. colleges and received some 34,000 responses. The poll asked seniors about their current religious preference. Later, in 1964, they were asked what this

preference had been when they entered college. The
two questions permitted determination of apostasy
rates in college.

In 1969, the American Council on Education
(ACE), acting for the Carnegie Corporation, polled
some 600,000 U.S. college students on various subjects, including religious preference as freshmen
and as seniors, which permitted determination of
apostasy rates in college.

In 1977 David Caplovitz and Fred Sherrow published an analysis and comparison of apostasy rates
based on the data from these studies. They reported
that "A comparison of college seniors in 1969 with
seniors in 1961 shows a sharp increase in apostasy
in each religion.... The Protestant rate in 1961
was 12%, and in 1969 17%." The Catholic rate rose
from 7% to 19% (Caplovitz and Sherrow, 1977: 164).
All of these rates reveal an intergenerational decline in faith.

They also reported that, among successive
classes of freshmen, Protestant apostasy rates rose
from 7% in 1966 to 14% in 1969; Catholic rates, from
3% to 13%; and Jewish rates from 13% to 15% (ibid:
175). Freshmen apostacy rates rose much faster than
senior apostacy rates (ibid: 177).

In 1968 NORC polled a 5000 person subsample of
the 34,000 seniors first polled in 1961, and repolled
in 1964. Caplovitz and Sherrow reported that the
three polls revealed a marked rise in apostasy rates
between 1961 and 1968. For Protestants, the rate
rose from 11%, to 12%, to 17% in 1968. For Catholics the corresponding rates were 5%, 8%, and 10%;
for Jews, 10%, 11%, and 8% (ibid: 160).

After reporting the above data, the authors
concluded that, "From the perspective of the religious communities in America, the most alarming data
we have presented are the trends toward apostasy
among entering college freshmen...for although apostasy undoubtedly grows during the college years...it
is also growing at a rather rampant rate among the
young before they reach college. Were this trend to
continue unchecked, it may well mean that in 50 years
of so, America's religious communities as we know
them today, will have disappeared" (ibid: 188).

24.   ACE Freshmen Religious Choice Data, 1968-82

Beginning in 1966 the American Council on Education (ACE) polled all entering freshmen in over
600 American colleges and universities on a variety

of subjects, including their current religious preference and that of their parents. The possible
answers were: Protestant, Roman Catholic, Jewish,
other, and none. In 1968, 9.6% of all students
replied "none." This figure rose to 14.3% in 1972,
and then fell to 9.8% in 1980, and to 8.7% in 1982.
However, the figure for "other," which probably includes many nonreligious persons (humanists, panthe-
ists, etc.) rose from 8.8% in 1968 to 16.5% in 1982.
As a result, the combined figure for the three more
orthodox religious groups fell from 81.6% in 1972 to
74.8% in 1982.

These ACE freshman data permit a revealing
comparison between the religious preferences of students and those of their parents. In 1968, 9.6% of
the students reported "none," while the like figure
for their religious background was 2.4%. In 1982,
the student figure was 8.7%, but that for their parents (average of father and mother) was 5.1%. The
figures for "other" showed much smaller but like
differences between students (1968, 8.8%; 1982,
16.5%) and parents (1968, 7.8%; 1982, 16.4%). These
comparisons clearly suggest a long-run decline in
religious faith because year after year, for 14
years, the freshmen were less religious than their
parents (ACE, 1968: 38; 1972: 34; 1980: 19; and
1982: 19).

25. Conclusions on Student Trends, 1914-74

All but 4 of some 40 studies or polls of trends
in student religious faith reviewed above report a
decline in religious faith. The four exceptions
suggest a cessation or reversal of the decline during
some period between 1940 and 1955 but all others reveal a net decline in the period they covered, which
varies from study to study. In the better U.S. non-
church colleges and universities covered by our studies, the percentage of students who firmly believed
in a personal God who answers prayers probably declined from over 65% in 1912 to less than 45% in
1974.

The decline in student religious faith from 1912
to 1974 would probably have been more rapid if there
had not been a vast expansion of college enrollments
during these years. This expansion substantially
lowered the average I.Q. of U.S. college students,
except in the elite schools, where the greatest
decline in religious faith occurred.

On the other hand, the vast expansion in the student population since 1912 has greatly increased the importance of this decline in faith. College alumni are now a far larger percent of the total U.S. population. By the year 2000 almost one third of U.S. adults will be college alumni, compared with less than 2% in 1910.

So far as I am aware, no scientific studies of trends in U.S. student religious faith after 1974 have been made. Unfortunately, Hoge has not replicated any of his 1967-68 polls, and no one else has done so. But it seems very likely that the decline in student religious faith has continued, especially among Catholics, because, as shown below, adult religious faith declined from 1968 to 1983.

The 1912-74 decline in student religious faith is very significant because today's students are tomorrow's religious and intellectual leaders. Moreover, as a result of aging, any trend in student opinion will soon become a trend in opinion among educated adults.

On the basis of our scanty data, we conclude that from 1912 to 1960, the rate of decline in U.S. student religious faith was more rapid among Jews than among Christians, and much more rapid among Protestants than among Roman Catholics (Zelan, 1968: 31; Allport et al, 1948: 13). Since 1960, however, the rate of decline has been much higher among Roman Catholics than among Protestants (Hastings and Hoge, 1976: 241-42; National Review, 1971: 640; Caplovitz and Sherrow, 1977: 164, 175).

The scant relevant data on the relative decline in religious faith among California students—Allport-Hoge, Wuthnow—suggests that the decline in U.S. student religious faith has gone much farther among California students than among other U.S. students. In sharp contrast, this decline seems to have been much slower in middle-west and southern states (Hunter). Additional data supporting these conclusions is given in the two following chapters.

Although not assembled and reviewed primarily for such a purpose, the data reviewed in this chapter—especially that reported by Leuba, Hoge, Rossman, and Wuthnow—strongly suggests that the long decline in U.S. student religious faith has been much more rapid, and has gone much further, among elite students in elite schools than among inferior students in third-rate schools. All available data relevant to this hypothesis is assembled and reviewed in the following two chapters. This additional data confirms the hypothesis.

C. The Decline in U.S. Lay Adult Faith

So far I have discussed only evidence on the trend in religious faith among U.S. college students. I turn now to evidence of the decline in U.S. non-clergy adult religious faith. I could find no previous review of this literature.

In beginning this review I return to Leuba because he was the great pioneer in the scientific study of trends in both student and adult religious faith.

1. Leuba's Study of Scientists, 1914-33

In both 1914 and 1933 Leuba queried over 1000 physical and biological scientists listed in the most recent edition of Cattell's American Men of Science (1910, 1933), and also polled about half of the teachers and researchers listed as members of the American Sociological Society and of the American Psychological Association, excluding only professors in Roman Catholic institutions, "a very small number." In 1914 he obtained useful answers from about 85% of those able to answer.

In both years he asked identical questions concerning: (1) belief in a personal God "to whom one may pray in the expectation of receiving an answer" which is "more than the subjective, psychological effect of prayer," and (2) belief in personal immortality, and permitted "yes," "no," and "no definite belief" answers (Leuba, 1950: 32-35, 44).

He reported that among his respondents the percent of belief in a personal God who answers prayers fell from 42 in 1914 to 30 in 1933, and that the percent of belief in individual immortality fell from 51 to 33 (ibid: 47).

These belief rates are much lower than those reported by Leuba for students in 1912 and 1933. Since changes in the beliefs of scientists and professors normally precede the foreshadow later changes in the beliefs of students, first, and the general public, later, Leuba's findings on the degree and trend of religious belief among scientists in 1914-33 clearly presaged the 1933-83 decline in student and adult religious faith.

Although the results of Leuba's research on religious trends among scientists were both startling and extremely significant, no one ever replicated his research work in order to confirm or disprove his findings. This is extraordinary and difficult to explain. Equally significant research in the natural sciences results in rapid efforts to confirm or disprove new and startling conclusions. The most plausible explanation for this neglect is public disapproval of Leuba's conclusions.

2. Steinberg on Carnegie-ACE Faculty Poll, 1969

In 1969 the Carnegie Foundation, collaborating with the American Council on Education, carried out a massive survey of some 400,000 college teachers, and included questions on religious background and current religious belief. In an analysis of the resulting data, Stephen Steinberg reported that the percent of those who were "traditionalists, i.e. orthodox and conservative in religious belief, varied directly, continuously, and markedly with age. For instance, he reported that 54% of Protestants over age 54 were traditionalists, and that the figure fell to 49% for age 45-54, to 38% for age 35-44, and to 33% for those under 35. For Catholics the decline was even greater, from 64% for the oldest, to 31% for the youngest professors (Steinberg, 1974: 142). These figures suggest a great decline in faith in one generation, i.e. from 1940 to 1969, the period in which some claim there was a revival of religious faith.

3. Catholic Digest Polls, 1952-1965

In 1952 the Catholic Digest hired Ben Gaffin and Associates to conduct a scientific public opinion poll of the religious views and practices of about 3000 U.S. adults age 18 plus. In 1965 another sample of about 4100 adults were asked the same question.

The polls revealed that the percent claiming to be "absolutely certain" that God (undefined) exists fell from 87% in 1952 to 81% in 1965. The percent who claimed they did not so believe rose from 1 to 2%. Among pollees age 18-24 the percent "absolutely certain" fell much faster, from 87 to 71%, but it fell at least 3 points in every age group. Among college graduates, it fell from 78 to 66; among Catholics, from 92 to 88; among Protestants, from 87 to 85; and among Jews, from 70 to 39% (Marty et al, 1968: 216-17).

These polls also revealed that the percent who think of God as a "loving Father who looks after us," i.e., as a personal God, fell from 79 in 1952 to 73 in 1965. Among adults 18-24, the percent fell from 80 to 67; among college graduates, from 63 to 47, and among Jews from 40 to 20 (ibid: 220).

These figures are far more significant than
those concerning belief in "God," undefined, because
the term God has so many different meanings—nature,
love, force, spirit, person, etc.—that many nonreligious persons can honestly claim to believe in
some kind of god. It is therefore especially noteworthy that, among young and educated adults, belief
in a personal God declined much more, and much faster,
than belief in "God," undefined. What the young and/
or educated believe today, the old and/or less educated will believe 50 years later.

In reply to a Catholic Digest question, "Do you
think there is a Heaven, where people who have led
good lives are eternally rewarded?" 72% of all adults
answered "yes" in 1952, and 68% in 1965. The percent
not believing in heaven rose from 25 to 28. For
Jews, disbelief rose from 70 to 83%. For college
graduates it rose from 33 to 40% (ibid: 248).

In reply to the question, "Do you think there
is a Hell, to which people who have led bad lives
and die without being sorry are eternally damned?"
58% of adults replied "yes" in 1952, and 54% in 1965.
For Catholics, belief fell from 74 to 70%; and for
Jews, from 15 to 3% (ibid: 250).

These polls also asked, "Do you believe the
Bible is really the revealed word of God; or...
only a great piece of literature?" Among all adults,
the percent answering "word of God" was 83 in 1952
and 79 in 1965. Among Jews, adults 18-24, and college graduates the rate of decline was over three
times as fast (ibid: 228).

4. The Overall Gallup-Poll Trends, 1944-84

Since 1944 the Gallup Poll (American Institute
of Public Opinion) has repeatedly asked U.S. adults
the bare and unrevealing question, "Do you belive
in God?" The "yes" answers were 1944 — 96%, 1947—
94%, 1954 — 96%, 1968 — 98%, 1975 — 94% (G. H.
Gallup, 1972, pp. 473, 698, 1293, 2174; G. H. Gallup,
1978: 627), and 1983 — 95% (S.F. Chronicle, 3-15-83,
p. 32).

A 1971 Gallup Poll on U.S. belief in God included two alternatives for the first time: (1)
belief in a "personal God" and (2) belief in a vital
force or spirit. The "yes" answers were 40% and 37%
(Gallup, 1972: 2311). The total for believers, 77%,
is so far below the average of four previous Gallup
Polls on belief in God, 96%, that it is suspect.
However, the newly reported breakdown by type of

-24-

belief is very significant. It revealed that, in 1971 20% of those who claimed to believe in "God" or a "universal spirit" actually believed only in a force of spirit, which might be impersonal.

In 1975, Gallup again offered pollees two alternative answers concerning their belief in God: (1) belief in God or a universal spirit, and (2) belief in a God or spirit "who observes your actions and rewards or punishes you for them." These questions differ from those asked in 1971, and the answers, too, differ. The combined figure for believers rose to 95%, and belief in a rewarding God or spirit, i.e., in a personal God, rose to 68% (G.H. Gallup, 1978: 627), far above the suspect 1971 figure of 40%. Unfortunately, Gallup has not repeated either the 1971 or the 1975 poll.

We conclude that the scanty and nonuniform Gallup Poll data on belief in some kind of God (undefined) reveal no significant trend between 1944 and 1975. But other Gallup Poll data do reveal significant trends in religious faith.

Gallup Polls on U.S. adult belief in "life after death" have yielded the following "yes" percentages: 1944 - 76, 1960 - 74, 1968 - 73, 1971 - 53, (H. G. Gallup, 1972: 474, 1663, 2174, 2311), and 1975 - 69% (G. H. Gallup, 1978: 627). The "no" answers rose steadily from 13% in 1944, to 31% in 1971, and then fell to 20% in 1975. The 1971 figures are suspect. These data reveal a marked decline in religious faith.

Theologians teach that religion can help us solve problems. In 1957, 1974, and 1981 Gallup polled Americans on their belief that "religion can answer problems." He reported that acceptance of this belief declined from 81% in 1957, to 62% in 1974, and then rose slightly to 65% in 1981 (G. H. Gallup, 1982a(61). The overall downward trend supports the conclusion that religious faith declined sharply from 1957 to 1981.

In 1952, 1965, and 1978, Gallup polled U.S. adults on how often they prayed. He reported that the percent of all adults who claimed to "pray more than once a day" was 38% in both 1952 and 1965, but fell to 27% in 1978. For adults age 21-24, the figures were 37%, 37% and 21% (G. H. Gallup, 1982b; 77). It is very significant that the figure for young adults fell much faster than the figures for all adults. Of course, prayer is a form of religious behavior, not an item of belief, but people do not pray in private unless they believe.

If religious faith has long been declining, adult public opinion polls with an age breakdown should reveal that the degree and amount of religious faith vary directly with age. In fact, all of them do so.

A 1944 Gallup Poll on belief in God (undefined) found that belief rose from 93% among those aged 20-29 to 97% among those over 50. Disbelief fell from 3% (age 20-29) to 1% (age 50+).

The same poll disclosed that belief in life after death rose from 70% (age 20-29) to 79% (age 50+) (G. H. Gallup, 1972: 474).

A 1981 Gallup Poll asked whether U.S. adults would "welcome" or "not welcome...religious beliefs playing a greater role in people's lives." Only 69% of those under 30 indicated that they would welcome this change, while 88% of those over 64 did so (G. H. Gallup, 1982b; 10).

The same poll allowed respondents to rate the importance of "following God's will" from 0 to 10. Only 39% of those age 25-29 gave it a 10 rating, while 65% over age 64 did so. And 8% of those aged 25-29 gave it a zero rating, compared with 2% for those over 64 (Ibid: 13).

A 1982 Gallup Poll on creationism versus evolution revealed that only 37% of U.S. adults age 18-29 believed in creationism, while 53% of those over 49 did so (G. H. Gallup, 1983a: 209).

In response to another 1982 Gallup Poll, 84% of pollees over age 64 reported that "I constantly seek God's will through prayer." For those under age 30, the figure was only 55% (G. H. Gallup, 1982b: 114).

In the same 1982 poll, 47% of pollees over age 64 claimed to believe that the Bible is the "literal word of God." Only 30% of those under 30 did so (ibid: 174).

A 1983 Gallup Poll on abortion found that 54% of pollees under age 30 approved of the 1973 U.S. Supreme Court ruling, while only 38% of those over age 64 did so (G. H. Gallup, 1983b: 17).

Some writers have conceded that young people are less religious in faith than old people, but have claimed that people become more religious in faith as they grow older. Therefore, they conclude, age differences in amount of faith do not prove that people are becoming less religious in faith. There are two major defects in such reasoning.

First, so far as I am aware, no one has ever
tested this claim by observing the changes in religious faith of a representative group of people throughout their lives. As explained in the next chapter,
age differences in amount of religious faith at any
given time are largely, perhaps entirely, due to
differences in amount of formal education.

Secondly, as revealed in this chapter, there is
abundant evidence that, from 1912 to 1938 and from
1958 to 1984, each generation of young people was
much less religious in faith than the previous generation. Therefore, even if each generation became more
religious as it grew older, each generation of old
people was probably much less religious than the
previous generation. There is no evidence, and little
reason to believe that the young - old gap in religious belief widened continuously and significantly
during these five decades.

6. Duncan on Detroit-Area Adult Polls, 1958-71

From 1952 on, the Detroit Area Study, carried out
at the University of Michigan, polled representative
samples of the Detroit area population on a variety
of issues, including some religious beliefs, in order
to train students in social research. In 1971 O. D.
Duncan, H. Schuman, and B. Duncan replicated parts of
the earlier polls in order to determine trends in
adult public opinion. They found that the percent of
those who "believe there is a God" (undefined) fell
from 96.6 in 1958 to 94.0 in 1971, and that the percent who answered "no" rose from 1.1 to 2.5%. Of
those who answered "yes," 68% were "very sure" in
1958; and only 48%, in 1971.

They also reported that the percent who believe
in "life after death" fell from 74 to 65, while "no"
answers rose from 14 to 22% (Duncan et al, 1973:
68-70).

According to Wuthnow, the Detroit area polls
also revealed that "the proportion very sure of God's
existence dropped 24 points for the younger group
[21-34] but only 15 points for the older group [35+]"
(Wuthnow, 1976: 856).

7. Wuthnow on S.F. Bay Area Study, 1943-73

In 1973 a 1000-person survey of the San Francisco Bay Area population (over 4 million) was made
as part of the Berkeley Religious Consciousness Pro-
ject. One purpose of this survey was to reveal

differences between the religious beliefs of subjects under and over age 35, and the survey revealed striking differences.

In a 1978 book, Robert Wuthnow reported that only 43% of subjects age 16-35 "definitely believe in God" while the figure for those over 35 was about 67%. Moreover, only 48% of the younger subjects "believe in creation," while 65% of the older subjects did so (Wuthnow, 1978: 134).

These data suggest a notable decline in religious faith in this area during the years 1943-73, and also suggest that this decline was likely to continue for another 40 years, as those under 35 in 1973 grew older.

8. NORC Catholic Polls, 1963-74

In both 1963 and 1974 the National Opinion Research Center of the University of Chicago interviewed a national sample of 927 Catholic adults on their weekly attendance at mass (1963 - 71%; 1974 - 50%), on monthly confessions (1963 - 37%; 1974 - 17%), acceptance of Catholic sex doctrines (1963 - 42%; 1974 - 18%), and on other indicators of religious faith (Time, 4-5-1976, p. 56).

While religious belief can change more or less than religious behavior, the above data on monthly confessions and on acceptance of orthodox sex dogmas suggest a rapid and radical decline in religious belief. Such rates of decline must be abnormally high, for a few more decades of such rapid decline would almost eliminate Catholicism in the U.S.

9. NORC Social Surveys, 1972-80

From 1972 to 1980 the National Opinion Research Center conducted "General Social Surveys," using samples of about 1500 U.S. adults. These surveys included several questions on religion, and the answers indicate a decline in religious faith.

Question #90, "In what religion were you raised?" yielded the answer "None" from 2.3 of all respondents in 1973, and from 3.0% in 1980.

In answer to question #86, "What is your religious preference?" 6.3% replied "none" in 1973, and 7.2% in 1980 (Davis, 1982: 89, 91). When the U.S. Census Bureau had asked the same question in 1957, only 2.7% had answered "none" (Glenn and Gotard, 1977: 444).

Each of these statistical series reveals a significant decline in religious faith in 8 years, but a comparison of the two is far more revealing. It shows that during each of two separate overlapping generations, the percent of U.S. adults having "no religion" more than doubled (from 2.3 to 6.3%, or from 3.0 to 7.2%). Only 2.3 or 3.0% of the parents were reported to have no religious preference, while 6.3 or 7.2% of the children claimed to have no such preference.

10. Ostheimer on Euthanasia, 1947-77

U.S. theologians and religious leaders have often harshly condemned active enthanasia, even when requested by painfully dying persons and their families. They assert that such behavior is a grievous sin. Thus the growing approval of such enthanasia is evidence of the decline of religious faith.

John M. Ostheimer has collected and reviewed the results of five national public opinion polls on active enthanasia "if the patient and his family request it." In three Gallup Polls the approval rate rose from 36% in 1947 and 1950, to 53% in 1973. An IOLI poll yielded a 52% approval in 1975, and a NORC poll in 1977 reported an approval rate of 62% (Ostheimer, 1980: 126).

11. Harris and Field Polls on Euthanasia, 1973-83

In 1973, 1977, and 1981 the Harris Poll asked adult Americans their views on active enthanasia for terminally ill patients. The percent who approved of such euthanasia grew from 37% in 1973, to 49% in 1977 and to 56% in 1981 (Hemlock Quarterly, Feb., 1982: 1).

In 1979 and 1983 the Field Poll asked a similar question of a representative sample of Californians. It found that the percent approving provision of life-ending medication grew from 58 to 68 in this four-year period (Hemlock Quarterly, Oct., 1983: 1).

12. Barrett's Estimates, 1900-1980

In 1981 Oxford University Press published a massive 1,010-page World Christian Encyclopaedia edited by the Rev. Dr. David B. Barrett, a Christian missionary in Africa. He had spent 14 years and visited 212 countries and territories collecting data on the religious affiliations and views of the entire world population. His encyclopaedia contains a separate statistical table for each nation, with figures for each religion and for nonreligious persons and atheists. His able discussion of methodology and sources suggest that his estimates should be given considerable weight.

Barrett's table, "Religious Adherents in the USA" (p. 711) reports that the number of "nonreligious" persons grew from 1.3% of the U.S. population in 1900 to 6.7% in 1980. For the decade 1970-80 the number of such persons grew by 501,700 a year, yielding an average annual increase of 4.05% and a 1980 total of 14,917,000.

He defined "nonreligious persons" as those who are unaffiliated and profess no religion or are agnostics (p. 836). He noted a Gallup report that in 1975 about half of nonreligious Americans were nonbelievers, and about half were completely indifferent (p. 713).

He gave separate estimates for atheists: 1,000 in 1900 and 400,000 in 1980. These figures are very dubious because they are so low and because the term atheist is ambiguous. He defined an atheist as one who denies the existence of any god (p. 817). If atheist is defined as a person without belief in any god, as it often is, it includes all agnostics.

Barrett estimated that the percent of Christians in the U.S. population fell from 96.4% in 1900 to 88.0% in 1980, and predicted a fall to 85.7% in 2000 A.D.

13.   Comments on Lay Adult Trends

From Leuba to Barrett, all the above 26+ scientific studies of the trend in U.S. adult religious belief support the conclusion that such belief declined steadily from 1912 to 1984. Believers have become less and less sure of their beliefs, and have increasingly abandoned religious dogmas. Moreover, the percent of nonbelievers has increased steadily. I have been unable to find any scientific studies which offer evidence to support contrary conclusions on these long-run adult trends.

The scanty evidence available clearly suggests that religious faith declined more rapidly among adult U.S. Protestants than among Roman Catholics during the first 60 years of this century, but that since about 1960 the rate of decline has been much more rapid among Catholics (Steinberg, 1974: 142; Time, 4-5-1976, p. 5).

In spite of the more rapid recent decline in
U.S. Catholic religious belief, U.S. Catholics
today are still more conservative in belief than U.S.
Protestants. Jews are much more liberal in belief
than Protestants.

D. The Decline of Faith Among U.S. Clergymen

1. The Betts-Hoge Clergy Polls, 1928-78

In 1928 George H. Betts (1868-1934), a professor
of Religion at Northwestern, sent a 56-item religious
faith questionnaire to 1309 Chicago area Protestant
"ministers in service" and received about 300 replies
(38%). He also sent the questionnaire to students in
five theological schools. According to Argyle (I
could not obtain Bett's report), Betts discovered
"very considerable differences between the replies of
the two generations. The students had much more
liberal ideas and tended to disbelieve in much traditional dogma. For instance, 47% of the ministers
believed that the Book of Genesis is literally true,
compared with 5% of the students; 71% of the ministers and 25% of the students believed in the Virgin
Birth; 60% of the ministers and 9% of the students
believed in the Devil" (Argyle, 1958: 31). These
data suggest a radical decline in religious faith in
a single generation.
  In 1978 Dean Hoge and John E. Dyble replicated
the Betts' study of ministers as closely as possible,
and reported the "median changes of six denominations" in answers to 54 questions. I shall note the
answers to only a few of the most relevant questions.
  Betts had asked, "Do you believe that God is a
being with personal attributes, complete and perfect
in all moral qualities?" Hoge and Dyble found that
the median decline in "yes" answers was 10 percentage
points (not 10%—he did not give 1928 and 1978 figures). They also reported a 14 point median decline
in belief "that the devil exists as an actual being."
  Betts had also asked, "Do you believe that
heaven exists as an actual place or location?" Hoge
and Dyble reported that the median decline in "yes"
answers was 17 percentage points. Belief in hell
suffered an identical decline, but, paradoxically,
belief "in the resurrection of the body" rose by 13
points, which implies a typographical error or gross
irrationality among respondents (Hoge and Dyble, 1981:
70-71).
  Hoge and Dyble averaged the answers to 48

questions on orthodox belief, and reported a 7 percentage point decline in the median "yes" answers for the 6 major denominations (ibid: 73).

2. J. K. Hadden, 1969

In 1965 Jeffrey K. Hadden sent a 524-item questionnaire to some 11,000 parish clergy of six major U.S. protestant denominations, and obtained usable replies from 7441. He asked them several questions about religious faith, and allowed six alternative answers, ranging from "definitely agree" to "definitely disagree." He classified his respondents into four age groups for each denomination.

He reported that, "In every denomination, younger clergy have a more liberal view regarding the interpretation of scripture than do older age groups. For example, only 14% of the Presbyterians under age 35 believed in a literal interpretation of scripture, compared with 31% of those over age 55 (Hadden, 1969: 51).

He reported similar but less radical differences between the opinions of young and old clergy on several specific doctrinal points. Thus he noted that 48% of Methodist clergy over 55 believed in the virgin birth of Jesus, but only 31% of those under 35 did so (ibid: 52-53).

His data strongly suggest that a 50-year decline in religious faith had occurred before 1965, and would probably continue into the future. He conceded that, as clergy become older, they may become more conservative, but claimed that "this interpretation... does not seem probable in this case" because "we found that older ministers who were educated in seminaries that were liberal 40 years ago are considerably more liberal than those...educated in more conservative seminaries" (p. 52).

3. The Decline of the U.S. Catholic Clergy, 1962-83

Nearly all public opinion polls on religious faith have revealed that American Catholics are more conservative in their religious beliefs than are American Protestants. It is therefore very significant that the Catholic Church has recently experienced increasing difficulty in keeping old priests and recruiting new ones. From 1962 to 1983 more than 12,000 U.S. priests turned in their collars, many to marry exnuns, and relatively few young men enrolled in Catholic seminaries. In 1962 the American church had some 48,000 seminarians, but by 1983 the number had fallen to less than 12,000. The average age of American priests was 56 in 1983, and is expected to rise to 73 by the year 2000 if recent trends continue.

Between 1965 and 1980 the number of religious sisters in the U.S. declined from about 180,000 to about 127,000, i.e., by about 27%, and the number of religious brothers fell from about 12,000 to about 8,600, i.e., by about 30% (Newsweek, 4-11-83, p. 70). These are large declines.

A 1984 study of the U.S. Catholic clergy, commissioned by the National Conference of Catholic Bishops, found that the number of entrants into women's religious orders fell from 32,433 in 1958-62 to 2767 in 1976-80, both being 5-year periods, and that the number of theology students preparing for the diocesan priesthood fell from 7855 in 1966-67 to 4244 in 1983-84 (San Francisco Chronicle, 12-14-84, p.40).

4. Gallup and Polling, 1960-80

In their book, The Search for American Faith (1980), George Gallup, Jr. and David Polling claimed that, "Throughout the current studies regarding the attitudes and convictions of the young clergy of America, a study of conservative image is being revealed. The younger clergy...believe firmly in the Adam and Eve narrative.... Some 70% affirm this view compared to 57% of the older clergy." Unfortunately, the authors did not name the "current studies" referred to, and did not give a source for the statistics they cited. Nor did they mention the well-substantiated contrary findings by Hoge and Hadden. Their book includes no bibliography. These facts and the tone of the book suggest that it is an example of religious apologetics rather than a scholarly contribution to knowledge.

The last page of this book displays charts showing U.S. adult changes during 1952-1978 in: (1) beliefs about Jesus, (2) the frequency of prayer, (3) belief in the importance of religion, and (4) reported religious training as a child. All suggest a decline in religion between 1952 and 1978. None of them support the authors' claim that "Recent studies demonstrate a powerful return to the conservative tenets of religion" (p. 133).

For instance, their chart on "religious training as a child" reveals that in 1952 only 6% of U.S. adults claimed to have had "none," while by 1978 the figure had risen to 17%.

-33-

E. General Conclusions on Decline in Faith

In this chapter I have: (1) reviewed some 40
studies or polls of trends in student faith, all but
four of which revealed a decline in religious faith
for some period between 1913 and 1972, and none of
these four reported a significant rise, (2) reviewed
about 26 studies or polls of U.S. adult religious
faith during the year 1914-83, all of which revealed
a decline in adult faith, (3) reviewed 2 studies showing a downward trend in religious faith among clergymen, and one dubious contrary claim, and (4) reported
a drastic decline in the numbers of the U.S. Catholic
clergy. Taken all together, these studies support
overwhelmingly the conclusion that U.S. religious
faith declined almost steadily during these years,
except perhaps from 1938 to 1958, and that the net
decline from 1914 to 1984 was substantial.
Another basis for this general conclusion is that
nearly all of some 90 studies of the effect of formal
education on religious faith, which I review in Chapter II, support the conclusion that religious faith
varies inversely and substantially with amount of
education. Since there was a continuous and, in total,
enormous growth of formal education during the period
1912-82, there was almost certainly a notable decline
in religious faith during this period.
My general conclusion of a decline in religious
faith includes the following more specific findings.
During the year 1912-82 the proportion of Americans
who were orthodox or traditional in their belief
declined almost continuously. Moreover, the number of
religious dogmas accepted by the typical religious
liberal also declined almost steadily. And the average intensity of belief in retained dogmas continued
to fall. Also, the proportion of Americans who were
agnostic or atheist increased almost continuously.
Finally, all of these three subtrends have gone much
further amont the young than among the old, among the
most educated than among the least educated, among
males than among females, and among the most intelligent and eminent adults than among their inferiors.
For instance, a 1982 Gallup poll on the origins
of the Bible revealed that the percent of those who
accepted the Bible as the "literal word of God" fell
continuously from 47% for pollees over age 64 to 30%
for those under 30. It fell from 56% for the least
educated to 21% for college alumni; and from 40% for
females, to 34% for males (Gallup, 1982b: 174).

Other recent Gallup polls on religious faith and/or behavior reveal similar differences. The differences due to variation in education and intelligence are fully covered in the next two chapters.

Since the chief subject of this chapter is the overall decline in U.S. religious faith, I have not reported data on regional differences in this trend, which might obscure the general picture, or distract the reader's attention from it. However, it is noteworthy that several recent Gallup polls on U.S. adult religious faith give regional breakdowns—east, midwest, south, and west. Nearly all of them reveal that the decline of adult religious faith has gone much farther in the east and west than in the midwest and south, and much farther in the midwest than in the south.

For instance, a 1982 Gallup poll on the origins of the Bible found that the percent of pollees who accepted the Bible as the "literal word of God" fell from 46% in the south, to 39% in the midwest, to 31% in the west, and to 30% in the east (G. H. Gallup, 1982b: 174).

Another 1982 Gallup poll, on creationism versus evolution, reported that belief in creationism fell from 49% of pollees in the south, to 46% in the midwest, and to 40% in both the east and the west (G. H. Gallup, 1983a: 209).

Some proreligious writers have criticized claims that religious faith has declined by calling attention to an alleged recent surge of Christian fundamentalism in the U.S. Therefore, I wish to emphasize that most of the polls on religious faith reviewed in this book have been polls on belief in fundamentalist dogmas, such as belief in a personal God, belief in life after death, and belief in creationism. The data from these polls provides much stronger evidence of a decline in fundamentalism than of a decline in religious liberalism. Indeed, it is possible that such liberalism, like atheism, has grown rather than declined during the past 100 years.

It may be objected that the evidence I have offered to support the conclusion that religious faith has been declining since 1900 merely proves that religious faith has changed, and become more sophisticated. There are two sound answers to this theory. First, a growing proportion of the population has become explicitly agnostic, positivist, or atheist. It is illogical to claim that a man who does not know whether he believes in God, or who claims that the term God is senseless, or who denies the existence of God is religious.

Secondly, people who believe in a personal God who answers prayers differ radically from those who believe only in an impersonal God operating through natural law and unaffected by prayer and worship. It is highly misleading and confusing to apply the term religious to both classes of people. The differences between their beliefs are much greater and more important than the resemblances.

I believe that nearly all opinion polls on religious faith in the U.S. yield data which overstate the real degree and extent of religious faith because most Americans are afraid of being called atheists, agnostics, or communists. In his comments on the religious faith of high school students in Elmtown, where he had carried out a social survey in 1947-48, A.B. Hollingshead (Yale) explained that, "to be labeled a church member is very important.... One can refer to himself as being of any Christian faith without inciting any opposition but....if he blandly says that he is an atheist, barriers will be erected around him by the devout, for atheist and communist are two labels an Elmtowner must avoid if he desires to be accepted as a respectable member of society" (Hollingshead, 1975: 181-82).

The American prejudice against atheists and communists is so well-known and so strong that Dean Hoge, the leading expert on past trends in American student religious faith, has suggested that it caused what he considered a pro-religious trend in U.S. student religious faith during the 1940's and 1950's (Hoge, 1974: 188).

I have demonstrated in this essay that nearly all relevant opinion polls support the conclusion that U.S. religious faith declined very substantially during the period 1912 to 1982. This was a trend from conservatism to liberalism in religious belief. I believe that this secularization was only a minor part of an overall trend towards more liberal ideas in all fields of social thought—in politics, morals, sex, race relations, sex roles, education, etc. This belief is based on my knowledge of recent history, not upon a careful review of relevant opinion polls. It is an hypothesis which ought to be tested by a thorough review of relevant polls. I hope that someone will soon make such a review.

F. A Contrary View — Caplow et al, 1983

Although the great majority of academic researchers on trends in U.S. religious faith have reported a decline in such faith, a few have denied the existence of such a trend. I have already noted the unpersuasive argument of George Gallup Jr., and David Poling. Now I wish to review the more recent and more detailed arguments of T. Caplow, H.M. Bahr, B.A. Chadwick, et al in All Faithful People, Change and Continuity in Middletown's Religion (1983).

In 1976-78 the authors replicated the Lynd 1924-25 social survey of a city they called Middletown (Munsie, Indiana), a survey which had included some questions on religious belief (see pp. 7-8 above). After reviewing the results of their replication, and other data, Caplow et al concluded that "we have not been able to find much trace of the great massive trend that was supposed to be carrying us irresistibly out of an age of faith into an age of practical reason. What has happened instead — the persistence and renewal of religion...is much more interesting than the secularization that never occurred" (pp. 37-38, my italics).

To support this unusual conclusion, they defined "secularization" as "a shrinkage of the religious sector in relation to other sectors of society," and described the religious sector as consisting of eleven forms of religious behavior, which they claimed had not declined (pp. 34-35). They not only ignored the evidence of other researchers (reviewed above, pp. 5-33) that such behavior had declined but, much more important, ignored most of the convincing evidence that religious faith had declined. For instance, they failed to refer to the research of Leuba, Katz, V. Jones, Hoge, Rossman, and most of the other researchers reviewed in this chapter. Indeed, they even asserted that "The only useful source of information about trends in religious beliefs...over an appreciable span of time that was available when we went to work in Middletown was George Gallup's 1976 report Religion in America" (p.26). I have summarized the results of 28 pre-1976 studies of the trend in U.S. religious faith "over an appreciable span of time."

The major fact that these authors ignored is the fact that Americans who engage in religious behavior today have much less religious faith than those who engaged in religious behavior one or two generations ago. They have simply ignored most of the evidence of such a decline in faith, and have implied that the persistence of religious behavior proves the persistence of unchanged belief in basic religious dogmas.

If they had restricted their conclusions to the trend in religious behavior, their conclusions would seem plausible, though controversial, but when, without reviewing the evidence, they claimed that there had been no decline in U.S. religious faith, they made a fatal and demonstrable error.

G. Church Membership and Attendance Trends

Those who doubt or reject the conclusion that U.S. religious faith has declined since 1912 are most likely to use statistics on religious behavior, including church membership and attendance. Therefore, a brief comment on such statistics is in order.

According to the Yearbook of American Churches church membership grew almost continuously from 15% of U.S. population in 1850, to 36% in 1900, and to 64% in 1964. These figures are grossly misleading, not only because, as the Yearbook editor explained, "the figures in the table for 1920 and prior years are not on the same basis as those for 1930 and the following years," but also because individual churches have used changing and widely differing methods of determining and reporting their membership, because they have failed to keep accurate records, and because the number of reporting churches has greatly increased.

Most historians report that in 18th-century Europe and North America the great majority of adults were church members. It is highly unlikely that U.S. church membership fell to 16% in 1850.

In 1832 William Ousely, a British consul in Baltimore, reported that American churches claimed over 12 million members out of a U.S. population of about 13 million. And in 1904, Max Weber, the eminent sociologist, estimated that "persons without church affiliation" amounted to only about 6% of the U.S. population in the 1890's (Lipset, 1959: 18).

Moreover, if there was a significant increase in reported U.S. church affiliation after 1850, it may have been largely due to more double-counting, to failure to drop apostates, to counting more wives and children as members, etc. For instance, Michael Argyle, an English sociologist, reports that "in the Episcopal Church in 1916 only 1% of its recorded members were children under 13, as compared with 26% in 1926." After adjusting for such factors, he concluded that U.S. church membership actually declined from 55% of persons over age 13 in 1906 to 51% in 1940, and then rose to 64% in 1950 (Argyle, 1958: 28).

In 1978 Daniel Rigney, Richard Machalek, and Jerry D. Goodman prepared and/or reviewed seven "indicators of religious change in the U.S., 1880-1972": (1) relative value of church construction, (2) relative amount of contributions to religion and welfare, (3) relative number of religious books published, (4) church membership, (5) church attendance, (6) relative number of religious degrees awarded, and (7) the percent of clergy in the work force. They reported that four measures revealed a secularization trend, and that "religious membership is the only measure to display a pattern of linear increase running counter to secularization... these data are highly suspect. Demerath... even goes so far as to suggest that if all methodological shortcomings were taken into consideration we might find real membership declines during periods of apparent growth" (Rigney et al, 1978: 386).

It is also very significant that there has been no appreciable increase in the percent of clergymen in the U.S. population since 1850, when it was 1.16 clergymen per 10,000 population (Lipset, 1959: 14). If the percent of church members grew from 16 to 64%, as the Yearbook claims, there should have been a continuous and rapid growth in the percent of clergymen in the U.S. population.

Gallup polled U.S. adults on church or synagogue membership repeatedly from 1936 to 1980, and reported an almost steady decline from 77% in 1936 to 69% in 1980 (Gallup, 1982: 16).

Gallup Polls have also revealed that the percent of U.S. adults who claimed to have attended church during the previous week rose from 41% in 1939 to 49% in 1955, and then fell to 42% in 1981 (G. H. Gallup, 1982b: 44).

Data collected by the Institute of Social Research of the University of Michigan reveal that "regular U.S. church or synagogue attendance rose from 38% in 1952 to 45% in 1964, and then fell to 40% in 1980, while the percent who 'never' attend rose from 8% in 1952 to 16% in 1980" (Benson, 1981: 580).

Finally, trends in church membership and attendance are poor indexes of trends in religious belief. Church members in 1980 were much less religious, i.e., less likely to accept traditional religious dogmas, than were church members in 1800, 1900, or 1950. Moreover, many persons who are not church members and/or do not go to church still believe in some religious dogmas.

H. Reasons for the Decline in Faith

Having proven that there has been a long decline in religious faith in the U.S., and probably in all advanced countries, I turn now to explain the reasons for this decline. The chief reason has probably been the growth of formal education in secondary and higher schools. The next chapter is devoted to a survey of the scientific public opinion surveys which have proven that, other factors being equal, every increase in the length of such formal education a person experiences tends to make him or her less religious, i.e., to weaken or reduce his religious faith.

In Chapter III, I review the like evidence which proves that religious faith varies inversely with native intelligence. It is unlikely that the average intelligence of the American people has increased since 1900, but the influence of the most intelligent Americans over American intellectual trends has increased greatly due to the rapid growth of both formal education and informal education from books, periodicals, radio and TV broadcasts, etc.

In the first part of Chapter IV, I discuss seven other major reasons for the decline of U.S. religious faith.

CHAPTER II

THE EFFECT OF EDUCATION ON U.S. RELIGIOUS FAITH

In an article on "The Future of Christianity and the Church" in The Futurist (Aug. 1970), Harvard theologian Harvey Cox noted that the French encyclopedists predicted that intellectuals would be the first to abandon religion. "Furthermore," he said, if they were right, "one would expect to find religion disappearing precisely in the most educated and cultured sections of the society.... this does not appear to be the case" (p. 122). Cox offered no statistical data to support this denial, and was apparently unaware of the many contrary findings by modern researchers.

There is much historical and literary evidence that faith in basic Christian and Jewish religious dogmas began its long decline over 300 years ago among the most highly educated men in the most advanced European countries, but only in this century has scientific statistical evidence to demonstrate the continuance of this trend been collected by scientific investigators, especially by public opinion pollers, in ever-increasing amounts.

In this chapter I review over 80 published religious opinion polls (all I could find) revealing the correlation between amount of formal education and amount or degree of religious faith among U.S. adults. The oldest poll covered is that of James H. Leuba, begun in 1912. The latest is a Gallup poll conducted in 1983.

Although the chief subject of this review is the relationship between education and religious faith, it covers some studies which dealt with a combination of religious faith and behavior because there is a high correlation between religious behavior and religious faith.

The best way to determine the correlation between amount of education and amount of religious faith is to poll a representative sample of the adult population on both the amount of their formal education and on their degree of faith in the most basic religious beliefs. Unfortunately, this has never been done. The majority of relevant studies have been made by college professors who have found it easy to poll captive students. But college students are not typical adults. Moreover, most of the religiosity tests used by college professors have been very incomplete and/or very poorly designed.

The most useful relevant studies of U.S. nonstudent adults have been conducted by commercial polling agencies, especially the Gallup organization, but these studies were designed to facilitate sale of the data collected, not to contribute to scientific knowledge. They usually cover one religious dogma only, and allow no report on intensity of belief. Nevertheless, the data they have collected is revealing and significant.

This chapter is divided into three main parts: (1) a review of studies of the religious beliefs of U.S. students, (2) a review of studies of the religious beliefs of U.S. college professors, and (3) a review of public opinion polls on the religious faith of U.S. adults. The studies of students began first, so I shall begin with them.

A. The Immediate Effect of Education on Student Faith

The decline of religious faith due to education normally begins in the early or mid teen years, well before students go to college, but unfortunately there is very little scientific evidence of this decline. College professors have often made scientific studies of the religious beliefs of their students, but few high school teachers have been both competent and free enough to so study their students. Therefore, I begin this essay with a review of studies, all but two of which (20 and 23) report the immediate effect of college education on students. The long-run effect will be covered largely in Section C.

The most recent and complete previous review of the literature on the immediate effect of college education on student religiosity is contained in a ten-page table (2E) in The Impact of College on Students, Vol. II (1969), by Kenneth A. Feldman and Theodore M. Newcomb. They summarized over 40 studies, including some unpublished studies and many on religious behavior, but covered only two pre-1936 studies, and, of course, none after 1969. In 1971 Clyde A. Parker published a review and summary of 29 such pre-1968 studies (Parker, 1971: 738-47).

The first modern scientific studies of the effect of education on religiosity were made by college professors who were familiar with the new applied science of opinion polling and who were able to practice it on students. The gifted path-breaking pioneer in this new and very important field of scientific research was Professor James H. Leuba of Bryn Mawr College, who began his polling of students on religious faith in 1906. His most significant polls occurred in 1914 and 1933.

1. Leuba, 1914, 1933

In both 1914 and 1933 James H. Leuba polled all students in College A, "of high academic rank and moderate size," on their belief in immortality. The response rate was 95% in 1914, and 90% in 1933. Each poll showed that belief in immortality declined between the first and the fourth year of college--from 80% to 70% in 1914, and from 42% to 27% in 1933 (Leuba, 1950: 49).

In 1933 he also polled all students in College B, of high rank and "radical in its leanings," on their belief in immortality, and got a 90% response. He found that their belief in immortality, declined steadily, and very rapidly, from 29% for freshmen to 5% for seniors (ibid: 30).

In 1933 he polled all students in both A and B on their belief in "a God to whom one may pray in the expectation of receiving an answer." In college A, belief declined from 34% among freshman to 20% among seniors; in B, from 20% to 5% (ibid; 27). These are large declines.

Leuba's data reveal that, perhaps by 1914, and certainly by 1933, most of the education-caused decline in student religious faith among the students he polled had occurred before they entered college. He was the first to discover this important truth, but he failed to call attention to it. Most later researchers also found that most loss of faith had occurred before students entered college.

2. E. S. Jones, 1926

In 1926 Edward S. Jones (University of Buffalo) published an account of his study of the opinions of 248 college freshmen, 76 upper class students, and 94 second-year law students. His 25-item questionnaire included five items on religious belief or attitude, including one on evolution and one on life after death. He reported that, "Religiously, the seniors tend to be far more liberal than the freshmen," especially on evolution and life after death, and that "women are distinctly more conservative" than men (E. S. Jones, 1926: 431-32).

3.   Bain, 1927

In 1924 sociologist Read Bain (University of Washington) gave a 17-item religious-faith questionnaire to 200 of his students (140 underclassmen, 30 juniors, and 23 seniors). He reported that "Leuba's conclusions that upperclassmen are more liberal than underclassmen is confirmed." Referring to male students, he concluded that "on all except a few questions the [16] seniors were more unorthodox than the other boys by substantial percentages." For instance, "On belief in God as a person, the Seniors show a percentage [of belief] of 7.1, while the other boys show 15.9" And 62% of the male seniors regarded Jesus as "human only," while only 38.2% of other male students did so (Bain, 1927: 764-65).

4.   R. H. Edwards et al, 1928

About 1927 R. H. Edwards, J. M. Artman, and G. M. Fisher polled several hundred seniors in 23 colleges and universities on a variety of issues including some religious questions. The students were selected because they were believed to be well-informed or leaders, and were individually interviewed. The researchers reported that the college experience had caused a significant change in religious faith. For instance, "in belief about the Bible, the largest groups were those who changed from a belief in the literal interpretation to a belief in the Bible as historical, allegorical or ethical (men 31%, women 35%)." (Edwards et al, 1928: 243).

5.   Katz and Allport, 1931

About 1928 Daniel Katz and Floyd H. Allport polled 1406 Wisconsin University students on their belief in a "Personal Creator, prayer as supplicating favor," and tabulated the answers by college class. They found that the percent of belief fell with each additional year of education from 25.8 to 20.6, to 19.6, and to 14.7% for seniors. By contrast, belief in an "Impersonal Spiritual Force...—no prayer" grew from 12.2% for freshmen to 19.8% for seniors (Katz and Allport, 1931: 268).

When Allport polled Harvard and Radcliffe students in 1946, he did not break down his results by college class, nor did he explain his failure to do so (Allport et al, 1948).

6. Garrison and Mann, 1931

About 1930, K. C. Garrison and Margaret Mann polled 258 male psychology-class students (40 freshmen, 51 sophomores, 105 juniors, 62 seniors) at North Carolina State College on their acceptance of 25 controversial statements, including 5 religious dogmas. Their questionnaire allowed students to give five different evaluations of each statement, ranging from "entirely true" to "entirely false."

For each of four religious dogmas, the percent of seniors who accepted it as "entirely true" was far lower than the percent of freshmen who did so. And for all five, the percent of seniors who rejected them as "entirely false" was far higher than the percent of freshmen who did so. For instance, 40% of the freshman, and only 21% of the seniors, gave the highest truth rating to statement (2), "Man was originally formed by a special creative act of God in a short time." And 29% of the seniors, but only 17% of the freshmen, rated this dogma as "entirely false."

Statement (8), "Christ was actually resurrected from the dead," was given the highest truth rating by 68% of the freshman, and by only 42% of the seniors (Garrison and Mann, 1931: 174). Apparently, most loss of faith occurred before college.

7. Wickenden, 1932

About 1931, Arthur C. Wickenden of Miami University polled 2990 entering freshmen and 966 near-graduation seniors in 20 schools in Ohio, Indiana, Michigan, Illinois, and Minnesota in order to determine the effect of four years of college education on student religious faith. Fifteen of his schools were "church colleges," and five were "non-church." He tabulated separate figures for each of these two groups. He asked 35 questions about concepts of God, and classified respondents in six classes, including "personal theists, impersonal theists, impersonalists, agnostics, atheists," and unclassifiable. He found that four years of college education was associated with a sharp decline in religious faith. For instance, the percentage of "personal theists" fell from 94% for freshmen to 82% for seniors in the 15 church-related colleges, and from 82% to 61% in the other five colleges. And the percent of "atheists" and "agnostics" rose from 1.0% of freshmen to 3.7% of seniors in church-related colleges, and from 3.7% to 7.9% in the other colleges (Wickenden, 1932: 261).

8. V. Jones, 1938 and 1970

In 1930-35, Vernon Jones gave the 20-item Thurstone-Chave Reality of God, form A, test to 381 Clark University male undergraduates, including 77 who were tested both as freshmen and as seniors. The range of possible test scores was zero to 11, with 11 indicating maximum faith. He reported an average test score of 7.07 for these 77 students as freshmen, and 5.54 as seniors. The decline of 1.53 was 4.94 times the standard deviation. A comparison of the average score for all freshmen with that for all seniors tested yielded a difference of 1.26, which was 6.0 times the standard deviation (V. Jones, 1938: 22).

In 1967-8 Vernon Jones again administered the same test to the entire Clark University freshman class (response 91%) and also to the senior class (response 67%). He reported that the difference between the average male freshmen and senior scores had fallen to .42 for men, and to .47 for women (V. Jones, 1970: 38). As the author noted (ibid: 36), the decline in the effect of college education between 1935 and 1968 was due to an increase in the loss of faith during high school. The 1931 and 1934 freshmen were much more religious in faith than the 1967 freshmen (ibid: 37).

In 1967 41% of the 369 freshmen claimed that "I trust in God to support the right and condemn the wrong," but only 33% of the 165 seniors did so. Also, 23% of the seniors reported that "God has no place in my thinking," but only 16% of freshmen did so (ibid: 39). Jones concluded that, "Seniors were found to be less favorable towards religion than freshmen in all the years studied" (ibid: 36).

9. Dudycha, 1934

In the fall of 1930, all freshmen at six small midwestern colleges were tested on their knowledge of and support for the theory of evolution. In the spring of the same year all seniors at seven similar schools (including five of those where freshmen also were tested) were given the same test, which allowed five degrees of assent to 25 propositions on evolution. In an analysis of the results, George J. Dudycha (of Ripon College, one of the schools included in both surveys) reported that "The Seniors...are ...more inclined to believe in evolution than the Freshman..." (Dudycha, 1934: 96). This is a gross understatement. The percent of believers in "evolution" rose from 23 to 61, and the percent who "absolutely do not believe" fell from 28 to 5 (ibid: 88.92).

10. Bugelski and Lester, 1940

In 1931, psychologists Richard Bugelski and Olive P. Lester polled over 200 University of Buffalo freshmen on 25 opinion statements previously used by E. S. Jones (including five on religious faith), and polled them again as seniors, three years later. They reported a "change in the direction of greater liberality" in all areas. "There is evidence on the set of religious questions considered separately, of change to a more liberal position," especially among members of "conservative sects" (Bugelski and Lester, 1940: 331).

11. Boldt and Stroud, 1934

In 1933 W. J. Boldt and J. B. Stroud administered M. H. Harper's Test of Social Beliefs and Attitudes to 738 students (411 freshmen, 106 sophomores, 98 juniors, 103 seniors, 20 graduates) of Kansas State Teachers' College, Emporia, in order to determine the effect of college education on student attitudes. The Harper test includes a group of pro-religious statements, and the answers to this group were separately tabulated. They revealed that the percent of "liberal," i.e., least pro-religious, answers for this group rose steadily from 30% for freshmen to 60% for seniors, and then fell to 39% for the 20 graduate students.
For instance, with respect to the claim that one should be guided by "the teachings of the Bible" rather than by experience and reason, the percent of liberal answers rose steadily from 38% for freshmen to 84% for seniors, and then fell to 65% for the 20 graduates (Boldt and Stroud, 1934: 616-17).

12. Symington, 1935

About 1934 Thomas A. Symington gave a Y.M.C.A. 100-item religious questionnaire to 504 students in

several high schools and colleges. He concluded
that, "Those who are more advanced at school or
college are more liberal in their religious thinking.
When 190 high school seniors and college freshmen
from the Eastern groups were compared with 216
Eastern college juniors, seniors, and graduates, the
advantage in favor of the latter [186 less 169, or
17] was very decided, the reliability of the difference being 12.2. When 57 college freshmen, sophomores, and juniors from the Western group were compared with 41 seniors and graduates from the same
colleges, the average [liberal] score in favor of
the latter [21] was again quite marked, the coefficient of the probable error being 7.2" (Symington,
1935: 43, 102).

13. Corey, 1940

In December 1934, S.M. Corey used the Thurstone-
Chave Reality of God scale in a poll of 234 University
of Wisconsin female freshmen. About a year later he
polled 100 of them (self-selected) again, using the
same scale. He found that his measure of their belief in the reality of God had fallen from 8.13 to
7.96 (SD = .98). This decline is too small to be
significant. The stability of belief shown is also
not significant (Corey, 1940: 346).

14. Nelson, 1940

In 1936 Erland Nelson (psychologist, Newberry
College) used the Thurstone-Chave Reality of God
Scale to reveal the religious beliefs of 3649 students in 18 colleges and universities. He compiled
separate data for eight classes of schools, but only
the first four classes had five or more students in
both the freshmen and the senior classes, so I shall
review only his findings for these four classes.
The Scale he used required students to rate
their degree of belief from zero to 11.0, and he
prepared mean scores for each class. He reported
that, among 1013 students in four state universities,
"Freshmen are most favorable toward the reality of
God [mean, 7.79] and seniors the least so [mean,
7.28] . The...difference is statistically significant" (Nelson, 1940: 375).
Nelson explained that a score of 7.0 or higher
expressed a belief in God, and on this basis he
concluded that 75% of his state university students
were believers. He claimed that this figure "is in

rather close agreement with that of Leuba" (ibid: 376). His data also showed that, by this criterion, 80% of his state university freshmen were believers, but only 70% of the seniors (ibid: 375). Clearly, most loss of faith occurred before college.

He found a "slight" increase in faith in the reality of God from the freshman year (mean 7.99) to the senior year (mean 8.09) among 1168 students in six Lutheran colleges (ibid: 377). However, this finding is far less significant than his finding for state universities because state university enrollments were more than 20 times as large as Lutheran college enrollments in 1936.

He reported that in three Friends Colleges 56 seniors were less believing (mean 7.84) than 188 freshmen (mean 8.05). His data for one Methodist university were very similar, freshmen 7.98, seniors 7.76 (ibid: 381).

15. Rankin, 1938

About 1937, Fay S. Rankin, a Ph.D. candidate at the George Peabody College for Teachers, polled 815 out of some 1800 undergraduates in four small southern colleges on their religious attitudes. About two thirds of the 77 items in his questionnaire were statements of religious dogma, the others being mostly favorable or unfavorable statements about religious people and behavior. All the items were chosen to help discriminate between religious liberals and conservatives. Subjects were allowed five possible responses to each item: "true, probably true, don't know, probably false," and "false."

Using a complicated, weighted scoring system, he found that the religious liberalism score rose consistently from 84.3 for 250 freshmen, to 90.3 for 204 sophomores, to 95.5 for 187 juniors, and to 96.8 for 128 seniors (Rankin, 1938: 33). He concluded that "There apparently is some tendency for the more educationally advanced groups to be slightly more liberal in their religious beliefs..." (ibid: 69).

He also compared the education of the parents with the religious views of the students, and found that the longer the education of the mother or father, the more liberal were the religious beliefs of the student. In his words, "There is some evidence that those students whose mothers are more advanced educationally are more liberal," and also that "those students whose fathers are more educationally advanced" are "more liberal" (ibid: 69-70). This was an important new discovery, one confirmed by later researchers.

Rankin's monograph contains a good review of the relevant earlier literature.

16. Gilliland, 1940 and 1953

A. R. Gilliland (Northwestern Un.) used the Thurstone-Chave Reality of God Scale to poll hundreds of his beginning psychology students in 1933, 1937, 1940, 1943, 1944, 1946, 1948, and 1949. In both 1933 (449 students) and 1937 (349 students) he reported separate mean scores for each college year. He concluded that in neither school year "was there a significant difference between the scores for any college year..." (Gilliland, 1940: 15). But his data revealed some secularization. In 1933, his mean score for 150 freshmen was 6.75, and the mean fell each class year, reaching 6.26 for 36 seniors. In 1937 the mean score for 217 underclassmen was 6.7, and that for 132 upperclassmen was 6.3 (Gilliland, 1940: 11-12).

In a later article covering his 1940, 1944, and 1949 polls, he reported that "there is some indication that juniors and seniors [mean, 6.8] are less religiously inclined than freshmen and sophomores [mean, 7.0] but this difference is small" (Gilliland, 1953: 115).

The smallness of these differences may be due to the fact that all his juniors and seniors were enrolled in a sophomore course. Moreover, the Thurstone-Chave Reality of God test is a poor test of religious faith because it asks about "belief in God" (undefined).

17. Hunter, 1942

In 1934, 1935, 1936, and 1937, psychologist E. C. Hunter of Converse College polled all freshmen (average class size 122) in a "small, southern, conservative, and religious college" for women, and later polled all survivors (38%) in their senior year. He used his own 94-item Test of Social Attitudes, designed to yield liberalism-conservatism scores, which included 10 religious items scored separately. He reported that, on these religious questions, "No appreciable changes in means from the freshmen to the senior year were noted" (Hunter, 1942: 246). Actually, there was a small but

statistically significant shift towards liberalism.
The average mean for all four years rose from -6.74
for freshmen to -6.45 for seniors (p. 248).

18. Gragg, 1942

In 1939-40 Donald B. Gragg of Hardin-Simmons
University studied the "religious attitudes" of 250
students in a small denominational college in the
"Bible Belt." He used the Thurstone-Chave reality
of God scale, and reported that the mean scores were
about the same (8.2, 8.3, 8.3, 8.4) for all classes.
The senior score was slightly and insignificantly
higher than that for any other class. He claimed
that his findings were similar to those of Gilliland
(Gragg, 1942: 258).
This abnormal result may be due to the defects
of the religious test used, or may imply that education in some small denominational Bible-belt
colleges does not reduce religious faith.

19. Arsenian, 1943

In 1938, 1939, and 1940 Seth Arsenian of Spring-
field College gave the Allport-Vernon Values test—
a poor test of religious faith — to all freshmen at
a small New England "professional school" where
"religious instruction and motivation find more em-
phasis than in most American colleges" (p. 339), and
later gave the same test to the surviving seniors.
This test included a religious belief section. He
reported that "The majority of students (75%) report
changes in concept of religion during four years of
college. The general direction of this change is
from formalistic and restricted to a more liberal
and encompassing understanding; from subjective,
personal, and contemplative to more objective, social, and active approach; from reverential and mystic
to rational and scientific viewpoint" (Arsenian,
1943: 348).

20. Kuhlen & Arnold, 1944

Several researchers have suggested that the
decline of religious faith among U.S. youth may now
proceed more rapidly during ages 12-17 than during
college years. However, very few studies of such
early changes in religious faith have been made.
One of the first was a study of changes between
ages 12 and 18 made by Raymond G. Kuhlen (Syracuse

Un.) and Martha Arnold (Goucher) about 1942. They polled 547 sixth, ninth, and twelfth graders (47% male, 24% Catholic) on 52 religious beliefs, permitting three reactions to each belief—"believe, not believe, wonder about."

The replies revealed a substantial to radical decline in belief in major religious doctrines, both from age 12 to 15 and from age 15 to 18. For instance, belief in a personal God "who watches you... and punishes you..." fell from 70% at age 12, to 49% at age 15, and to 33% at age 18. Disbelief rose from 18, to 37, to 48%. The percent believing that "every word in the Bible is true" fell from 79, to 51, to 34%. However, belief that "there is a heaven" declined much more slowly—82, 78, 74—as also did belief that "prayers are answered"—76, 69, 65 (Kuhlen and Arnold, 1944: 293).

21. Allport, Gillespie, and Young, 1948

In 1946, G. W. Allport, J. M. Gillespie, and J. Young of Harvard polled some 500 Radcliffe and Harvard undergraduates on their religious views, and included questions on current religious preference and on their religious background. The answers of 389 Harvard students revealed that 30% of those with a religious background now believed that they had no need for religion (17%), or were doubtful about such a need (13%). Although 44% had been reared as Protestants, only 18% still chose this faith. For Catholics, the figures were 16% and 11% respectively; for Jews, 17% and 6%. The only faith to gain adherents was "ethical but not theological Christianity" (4% to 11%), and this too reflects a decline in religious faith (Allport et al, 1948: 13).

This test does not permit us to determine how much of this loss of faith occurred in high school and college, but much of it probably occurred then.

22. Fortune-Roper, 1948

In 1948, Fortune, the magazine, hired Elmo Roper, the professional poller, to conduct a national survey of American youth. The survey included one question on religious faith, "Do you think there is a God who rewards and punishes after death?" Respondents were classified by amount of education—grade school, high school, some college, and college alumni. The percent who answered "yes" fell from 78 for both the grade school and high school groups

to 60 for college students. Much more significantly,
the percent who answered "no" rose rapidly and consistently from 8, to 13, to 35% for these three groups
(Fortune, Dec., 1948: 44).

23. Remmers and Radler, 1957

In 1942-57, Purdue University sociologists conducted a national survey of the opinions of some
18,000 high school students. Their poll included ten
statements about evolution and other religious beliefs
and attitudes. In an analysis of the resulting data,
H. H. Remmers and D. H. Radler reported that "Responses to these statements indicate that high school
seniors, at least in some respects, have moved closer
to the orthodox end of the [orthodox-secular] continu-
um". For instance, rejection of the theory of evolution rose from 35% of the freshmen to 44% of the
seniors. And "6% more seniors than freshmen believe
their fate in the hereafter to be determined by their
conduct on earth" (Remmers and Radler, 1957: 158).
These findings differ radically from those of Kuhlen
and Arnold, and are contrary to most findings on the
effect of education on religious faith. Remmers
and Radler did not mention the contrary findings of
Kahlen and Arnold, which had been published 13 years
earlier.
Later in this chapter I review several Gallup
adult polls which consistently reveal that high school
alumni who do not go to college are less religious
in faith than adults with no high school education.
These polls strongly support the conclusions of Kuhlen
and Arnold on the effect of high school education on
U.S. religious faith.

24. Hastings and Hoge, 1948, 1967, 1974

In 1948, Phillip K. Hastings polled 92 male
Williams College undergraduates on their religious
backgrounds and on their current choice of religious
tradition. The poll was repeated on 205 male students
in 1967, and on 210 students in 1974. The authors
reported that in both 1967 and 1974 there was a "lack
of change in religion from college class to college
class.... Apparently the effect of intellectual
training on students' religious views occurs more
during high school today than several decades ago"
(ibid: 247). But it is not clear that "change in
religion" means "change in religious belief." Moreover, Leuba had shown that in 1933 most loss of faith

occurred before college.

They noted that their conclusion on the effect of college education differed from those of previous investigators, mentioning Mary C. Van Tuyl and Paul B. Horton. I have been unable to secure the Van Tyle and Horton articles.

In an earlier report on the 1948 and 1967 Williams polls, Hastings and Hoge had reported that "higher parents' education is associated with a more liberal student religious orientation" (Hastings and Hoge, 1970: 26).

25. Vinacke, Eindhoven, and Engle, 1949

In 1948 psychologists W. E. Vinacke, Jan Eindhoven, and J. Engle of the University of Hawaii used a slightly modified form of the Allport, Gillespie, and Young 1945 Harvard questionnaire to test 577 UH students, 40% of Buddhist background. Students were asked concerning any change in religion. The authors reported that, "As at Harvard, students at Hawaii markedly tend to shift their religious choices towards more "liberal" positions. Thus we find that, in addition to those who choose liberal Protestantism or Ethical Christianity, 7% say that some new form of religion is required. There is also a marked increase in those who reject religion or are doubtful about any need for it..." Moreover, "We find that only 8% of the men and 14% of the women believe their faith is more firm than their mothers' (7% and 14% at Harvard and Radcliffe)..." (Vinacke et al, 1949: 168).

Since they too tested their students only once, and did not give separate results for different school years, we cannot tell how much of this great liberalization occurred during college.

26. Ross, 1950

About 1948, M. G. Ross polled some 1900 Young Men's Christian Association members (age 18-29) in the Northeastern states of the U.S. on their religious beliefs and affiliations, and on the amount of their education. He reported that the members with the most education were the least religious. For instance, he found that only 28.6% of the 364 college graduates believed in a God, who is "personal" and "may be appealed to through worship and prayer." The percent rose to 35.5% for 585 members with some college education, and to about 43% for those with no college education (Ross, 1950: 22). Belief in personal immortality rose from 36.1% for college graduates to 49.9% for part-college alumni, and to about 60% for those with no college education (ibid: 52).

27.   Brown and Lowe, 1951

In 1948 Daniel G. Brown and Warner L. Lowe polled 613 protestant students in lower-division liberal arts courses at the University of Denver on their belief in 15 Christian doctrines, and classified the replies by college class. They reported that "A significant decrease in the mean scores of religious belief was found from freshmen [49.9] to sophomores [46.6], from freshmen to juniors [43.1], from freshmen to seniors [43.4], and from sophomores to juniors" (Brown, 1951: 114).

Brown and Lowe noted that their results disagreed with those obtained by Gilliland and Gragg, and explained this by noting that they, like most other researchers in this field, had studied students in a nondenominational school, while Gragg and others had studied students in denominational schools.

28.   Webster, 1958

During this years 1953-57, 274 Vassar College students were given the same personality tests both as freshmen and as seniors. Several of the 123 test items concerned religious faith or behavior, and answers to all of them revealed a considerable reduction in such faith or behavior while at Vassar. For instance, in 1953, only 39% of the freshmen denied belief "in a life hereafter," while 53% of the same students did so in 1957. And only 10% denied belief in "a God" in 1953, while 25% did so in 1957. Also, in 1953, only 16% claimed to be agnostic, compared with 35% in 1957. The percent who denied going to church "almost every week" rose from 50 to 72%, and the percent who denied praying "several times a week" rose from 36% to 57% (Webster, 1958: 112-13).

29.   Bryant, 1958

In 1958 M. D. Bryant submitted a Ph.D. thesis at the University of Nebraska, Patterns of Religious Thinking of University Students as Related to Intelligence. It was based upon a poll of 52 matched pairs of freshmen and senior students. I have not read his unpublished thesis. According to Feldman and Newcomb, Bryant found that the seniors were more liberal than freshmen in their religious beliefs. For students of "average intelligence" the liberalism score rose from 8.26 to 10.50. However, his intellectually superior freshman had a liberalism score of 9.96, the same as that for them as seniors (Feldman and Newcomb, 1969: 31).

30. Young, Dustin, and Holtzman, 1966

In 1955, 1958, and 1964, Wayne H. Holtzman, Robert K. Young, and their associates (Un. of Texas) used a 23-item questionnaire to measure changes in "attitudes towards organized religion" among 500-600 UT undergraduate students (a 5% random sample). They reported that, in 1958, 128 freshmen had a mean score of 65.2, while 120 seniors had a mean score of 59.4. In 1964, 146 freshmen scored 57.1, compared with 54.4 for 131 seniors. Thus the religious score varied inversely with length of education in both years. However, in 1964, but not in 1958, the religious score rose for fifth-year students, who numbered only 33. In 1958 the scores continued to decline for the 43 fifth- and sixth- year students (Young et al, 1966: 43).

31. Putney and Middleton, 1961

In 1959 sociologists Snell Putney (San Jose State) and Russell Middleton (Florida State) polled 1126 Christian students enrolled in social science courses at 13 colleges and universities in New York, New Jersey, Pennsylvania, Florida, and Georgia on their religious attitudes. They designed their own "orthodoxy scale" consisting of six statements of religious faith, and allowed seven possible responses, ranging from strong agreement to strong disagreement. This permitted a possible score range of 6 to 42. They reported a negative correlation of -.24 ($\pm$ .05) between religious orthodoxy and year in college (Putney and Middleton, 1961: 288).

32. Havens, 1964

In 1959 Joseph Havens of the University of Massachusetts polled 188 UM students (20% of each college class) on their religious views, using the 25-item M. D. McLean questionnaire on religious orthodoxy. In 1962 he repeated the test for like numbers of freshmen (62) and seniors (39). He reported that

the proportion of orthodox believers fell from 28%
to 3% between the freshmen and senior classes in
1959, and from 37% to 15% in 1962. The percent of
"nonreligious" rose from 24% to 36% in 1959, and
from 32% to 36% in 1962. Those classified as
"liberal" grew much faster, from 29 to 53% in 1959,
and from 26 to 46% in 1962 (Havens, 1964: 82). These
data reveal a radical loss of faith before college.

33. Webster, Freedman, and Heist, 1962

About 1960 the Center for the Study of Higher
Education (UC, Berkeley) asked 470 National Merit
Scholarship winners in a wide variety of colleges
"Do you personally feel that you need to believe in
some sort of religious faith?" The same students
were polled on entering college, & at the end of the
first, second, and third years. During these three
years, the proportion of affirmative answers fell
continually for 395 men from 88% to 70%, to 61%, to
51%. For 175 women the corresponding figures were
91%, 76%, 74%, and 69% (Webster et al, 1962: 826).
These data suggest a marked decline in religious
faith among these very superior students during
their first three years at college.

34. Glock and Stark, 1966

In 1958 the National Opinion Research Center
polled 2842 graduate students in 25 U.S. Ph.D.-
granting universities on their religious affiliations. In 1965 Charles Y. GLock and Rodney Stark
(U.C., Berkeley) analyzed the data obtained in this
NORC poll. They reported that while only 7% of these
students had parents who had no religious affiliation, 25% of the students had none in 1958. The
authors also noted that the U.S. Bureau of the Census
had reported that only 3% of the U.S. population had
no religious affiliation. They concluded that "a
major religious phenomena associated with being a
graduate student is a loss of faith" (Glock and
Stark, 1965: 269-71). The most plausible explanation for this "loss of faith " is the formal education these students had received.
These NORC data report religious affiliation,
not religious faith, but I agree with the authors
that "there seems some basis for interpreting...
reports of no religious preference as implying a
rejection of religious beliefs" (ibid: 270), especially since the reported differences in religious

affiliation were so large.

35. Hadden, 1963

A 1961 study of 261 University of Wisconsin seniors yielded data which enabled Jeffrey K. Hadden to find that the religiosity of these students varied inversely (-.18) with the amount of their fathers' education. He reported that "persons who were low on conventional religiosity were more likely to have fathers who had attended college" (Hadden, 1963: 214). The most plausible explanation for this is that the children of more educated parents become better educated than children of less educated parents. Better home education supplements formal education. Another partial explanation is that children of better educated fathers have higher IQs than other children.

The fact that college-educated parents have children who are less religious than other children implies that the college education of the parents had a permanent liberal effect on the parents' religious views.

36. Lehman, MSU, 1958-62

In May, 1962, Irvin J. Lehman (Michigan State) retested 1,051 MSU seniors whom he had first tested as entering freshmen in September 1958. He asked all seniors, "In what ways are you now different from what you were as a freshman?" and specified 39 ways in which they might have changed, including four ways relating to religious belief: (1) "acceptance of the Bible as a guide to...living," (2) "attachment to a religious sect or denomination that I can believe in..." (3) "feeling of the necessity for religious faith..." and (4) "commitment to a set of religious beliefs."

He reported that in ways (1), (2), and (4) the percent of students who reported they had become less religious was 50 to 200% larger than the percent who reported they were more religious. For instance, 34% of the men had become less accepting of the Bible as a guide, compared with 11% more accepting. For women, the figures were 31% and 13% respectively. On commitment to a set of religious beliefs, the figures were 34% and 20% for men, and 33% and 24% for women (I. J. Lehman, 1963: 313-14).

Only with respect to feeling the necessity for religious faith did seniors report they were more religious: men 33% to 29%, and women 23% to 40% (ibid: 312). But these data may reflect growing interest in and need for a liberal religious faith, perhaps deism or humanism, because the term religious faith covers a very wide range of religious, philosophic, and scientific beliefs. Therefore, the implication of these data is undeterminable.

37. Toch et al, 1964

In both the Fall of 1960 and the Spring of 1962 H. H. Toch, R. T. Anderson, J. A. Clark, and J. J. Mullin (all of Michigan State Un.) gave the same 101-item religious-belief tests to the same 120 MSU students, who had been freshmen in 1960. They found that 19 of the 101 items evoked the highest response differences between 1960 and 1962. For all these 19 items the answers revealed a decline in religious faith, in most cases a very marked decline, after only a year and a half of college. For instance, the percent who agreed that "Every word in the Bible is divinely inspired" fell from 29 to 14. The percent who agreed that "God is a product of man's wishful thinking" rose from 7 to 15. And the percent who agreed that "Man is headed for destruction; only God's miraculous intervention can save us" fell from 28 to 15 (Toch et al, 1964: Table 3).

38. Hites, 1965

In 1956, psychologist Robert W. Hites (Birmingham Southern) gave all incoming BS freshmen a religious poll including 37 Likert-type religious questions. The same poll was used again in 1960 on all 60 students still in school.
He segregated the results for those questions relating to "liberal-nonliberal acceptance of the Bible," and reported that the change in attitude on this subject from freshmen to seniors "represents a movement from a more literal to a less literal interpretation of religion..." (Hites, 1965: 56).

39. Trent, 1967

In 1959-64 James W. Trent, then a graduate student at U.C. (Berkeley), studied over 4000 freshmen and seniors—including 618 both as freshmen and seniors—at five West Coast Catholic colleges, S.F. State College, and U.C. (Berkeley). He gave them the

Religious Liberalism Scale of the Omnibus Personality Inventory. He classified the 618 retested
students as "Catholic," "Secular Catholic" (who
attended non-Catholic colleges), and "Non-Catholic."
    He reported that the mean liberal religious
score for the 321 non-Catholics rose from 51.2 in
their freshman year to 56.2 in their senior year.
For the 54 secular Catholics, the mean score rose
from 41.0 to 48.0. Even the Catholics who attended
Catholic colleges became more liberal, i.e., less
religious, their score rising from 35.5 to 37.8
(Trent, 1967: 190). Since U.S. Protestant and
"Secular Catholic" students outnumber U.S. "Catholic"
students over five to one, the first two comparisons
are much more significant than the third.

40. Clyde A. Parker

    About 1968, Clyde A. Parker (Un. of Minnesota)
reviewed 29 studies (5 unpublished) "which attempted
to assess change in religious beliefs during college." They were made in the years 1928-67. He
reported that 17 of these studies "report data which
show change from orthodox or conservative beliefs to
liberal or secular ones. Only one study reported
data in the opposite direction" (Parker, 1971: 737).
Most of the other 11 studies did not deal with changes in belief in religious dogmas, but with attitudes toward church or religion, need to believe,
religious knowledge, etc.

41. Feldman, 1969

    In 1969 Kenneth A. Feldman and Theodore M.
Newcomb reviewed nearly all of the 1936-1968 literature (38 polls) on the impact of college education on
religious faith and reported that "These studies show
that...seniors are somewhat less likely to believe in
God and more likely to be indifferent or opposed to
religion, are somewhat more likely to conceive of
God in impersonal terms, are somewhat less orthodox
or fundamentalistic in religious orientation, and
are somewhat more religiously liberal" (Feldman and
Newcomb, 1969: 32).

42. Wuthnow and Glock, 1970-71

    In 1973 Robert Wuthnow and Charles Y. Glock
published an analysis of some of the data on student
religious orientation collected by the Institute for

Research in Social Behavior (Berkeley) in a 1970-71
survey of the values of some 2000 University of
California male freshmen and senior students. They
reported that 47% of the 960 freshmen and 52% of the
986 seniors classified themselves as "agnostic,
atheist, or as having no religion" (Wuthnow and
Glock, 1973: 160), which suggests that four years of
college weakens religious faith. However, the fact
that 47% of the freshmen claimed to have no religious
faith, while only 19% came from nonreligious families
(ibid: 163) reveals that most student loss of faith
had occurred before entering college, and was probably due to high school education, personal reading,
and a high IQ. Like the Hastings-Hoge Williams
College study, this study suggests that very superior students now lose most of their religious faith
in high school rather than in college.

43. Chandler-CBS, 1972

In 1969 the Columbia Broadcasting System commissioned Daniel Yankelovich, a professional poller, to
conduct a national survey of both college and noncollege youth. According to Robert Chandler, who
wrote a book on the results, "the survey confirmed a
shift of major proportions in youthful attitudes...
towards sex, drugs, religion..." (Chandler, 1972:
53).
Moreover, it revealed that the college youth
were much less religious than the like-age noncollege
youth. For instance, 17% of the college youth checked the statement, "I'm an agnostic. Religion plays
no role in my life," while only 8% of the noncollege
youth did so. And only 13% of the college youth
claimed that "religion plays an important role" in
my life, while 22% of the noncollege youth did so
(ibid: 62).

44. Argyle and Beit-Hallahmi, 1975

After reviewing the evidence available in 1975
concerning the effect of education on U.S. student
religiosity, M. Argyle and B. Beit-Hallahmi concluded
that "If the overall average changes are examined,
there is a highly consistent trend towards a lower
level of church attendance and a lower level of
religious beliefs and attitudes. These studies show
that students in their later years are less orthodox,
less fundamentalist, less likely to believe in God
and to think of him as a person..." (Argyle and Beit-
Hallahmi, 1975: 34).

45. Gallup Polls, 1976

In a nationwide poll in 1975, Gallup asked U.S. college students, "Do you believe in God or a universal spirit?" allowing "yes, no," and "don't know" answers. The percent of "yes" answers fell continuously from 93% for freshmen to 81% for seniors. The percent of "no" answers rose continuously from 4% for freshmen to 11% for seniors.

The students who answered "yes" were then asked if they believed in a God or spirit who "observes your actions and rewards or punishes you for them." Only 52% replied "yes," as compared with 68% for all U.S. adults. Among students this figure fell each class year, from 59% for freshmen to 43% for seniors.

In the same poll, all students were asked, "Do you believe in life after death?" Of the freshmen, 72% replied "yes." and 23% "no." Of the seniors, only 62% said "yes," and 29%, "no" (G. H. Gallup, 1978: 639-40).

In this Gallup poll, students were also asked: "Do you believe a woman should be able to have an abortion under proper medical supervision if she wants to, or should it be permitted by law only under certain circumstances?" The poll revealed that only 55% of freshmen approved the first alternative, abortion "if she wants to," but the figure rose to 64% for sophomores, and to 71% for seniors.

46. Caplovitz and Sherrow, 1977

One very significant effect of college education on religious faith is that it causes many students to abandon their parental faith and adopt no other religious faith. Caplovitz and Sherrow call such behavior becoming apostate. For them "apostasy indicates...loss of religious faith..." (Caplovitz and Sherrow, 1977: 30-31).

In 1961 the National Opinion Research Center polled some 34,000 seniors in 135 U.S. colleges, and included questions on both current religious preference and that of parents. Three years later they asked the same respondents to report their religion when they entered college. Together these polls permitted Caplovitz and Sherrow to determine the effect of four years of college on apostasy. They reported that apostasy rates grew during four years of college as follows: for Jews, from 4 to 13%; for Protestants, from 5 to 12%; and for Catholics, from 2 to 7% (ibid: 109). They also noted that, for all religious groups, apostasy rates grew much less rapidly among students who lived at home than among those who lived away from home. Thus, "greater involvement in college life is conducive to apostasy." This implies that loss of religious faith while at college is not due to aging.

In 1969 the American Council of Education, acting for the Carnegie Corporation, polled over 600,000 college students on a variety of issues, including religious affiliations. Caplovitz and Sherrow analyzed the religious data, and reported that apostasy rates rose with each additional year in college, most rapidly for Catholics--10, 14, 16, and 19%—and least rapidly for Protestants—15, 17, 17, and 17%.

These figures reflect the effect of both precollege and college experience. To determine the effect of college only, we must deduct the apostasy rates of these students when entering college, rates which rose rapidly from 1966 to 1969. If this is done, it appears that the 1969 Protestant senior and junior apostasy rates were both 10 points higher than the 7% rate for their class on entering college, while the 1969 sophomore rate was 8 higher (ibid: 175).

Caplovitz and Sherrow concluded both that "The more years spent in college, the greater the loss to the religion of origin," and that "between 1965 and 1969 those starting college were more and more likely to be apostates" (ibid: 176). In fact, apostasy grew very much faster during high school than during college from 1966 to 1972 (ibid: 177).

47. Comments on Student Studies

I have now covered over 50 polls revealing the correlation between amount of education and amount of or change in religious faith among students in many different schools and regions of the U.S. All but two of them (Gragg, Remmers and Radler) found evidence of a negative correlation between amount of education and student religious faith, and only Remmers and Radler reported a significant positive correlation, and only for high school students. Some of the negative correlations reported were not statistically significant, but the sum total of these findings is clearly statistically significant, and much more so than any individual finding.

The student polls and studies reviewed in this chapter strongly supoort one major conclusion, namely that every additional year of undergraduate college education is associated with, and probably the major cause of, a decline in the amount and/or intensity of religious belief among American college students and alumni. They also suggest, less strongly, that each year of postgraduate university education has a similar effect. Thirdly, three studies (Rankin, 1938; Hadden, 1963; Hastings, 1970) reveal that, among like-year U.S. College students, the amount of religious faith varies inversely with the amount of education of the parents, which implies that the effect of college education on religious faith continues through at least two generations.

Perhaps the most surprising fact revealed by student opinion polls is that most American student pollers had experienced a marked loss of religious faith before entering college. The more prestigious the college, the greater the precollege loss of faith. For students in some elite schools, the precollege loss of faith was greater than the loss during four years of college. And this has been true since 1933 at least, and perhaps much longer.

Stephen M. Corey (Un. of Nebraska) and others have suggested that the difference in religious faith between freshmen and seniors may be due to the fact that many freshmen drop out of college before graduation (Corey, 1936: 327). However, I have reported 8 studies (V. Jones, Hunter, Arsenian, Hites, Webster, Lehman, Toch, Trent) which compared the faith of the same student during their first and fourth college years, and all but one showed a decline in religious faith.

48. Student Trends as Evidence of Adult Trends

All of the religious faith data and conclusions discussed so far in this chapter deal with students, but for several reasons, this data strongly suggest that there was a long parallel decline in religious faith among U.S. adults.

First, it is socially and statistically highly unlikely that student religious faith could decline for several decades without a similar decline among adults. The opinions of students, especially college freshmen, have been largely determined by those of their parents and other adults. And there is much evidence that freshman religious faith declined even more rapidly than senior religious faith from 1912 to 1975.

Secondly, several student polls revealed that students claimed to be less religious in faith than their parents, some of whom when students had claimed to be less religious in faith than their parents. For instance, the students polled by Leuba in 1912-14 may have been the parents of some students he polled in 1933. And if not parents, they probably closely resembled such parents. And the students of 1933 became or resembled the parents of 1960. In each generation the students claimed to be less religious than their parents and/or average adults, but there is no evidence that this difference grew during the period 1912-70. Indeed, it seems to have narrowed, because the decline in freshmen faith, most influenced by parent faith, was more rapid than that in senior faith, most influenced by education.

Thirdly, there is no reliable evidence that college alumni become more religious in faith as they grow older. Therefore, if each generation of college alumni is less religious in faith than the previous one, each generation of educated adults and parents should have less faith than the previous one.

Some students have reported that, at any given date, old people are more religious in faith than young people, but this does not prove that people become more religious as they grow older. I believe I have provided convincing evidence that, at any given time, old people are more religious in faith chiefly because they are less educated than young people.

Finally, during the years 1912-75 the proportion of college alumni in the total U.S. adult population grew steadily, so that their religious views became ever more determinative and typical of the views of adults in general. In the near future, college alumni will make up over one third of the U.S. adult population. Thus it has long become ever more likely that trends in religious faith among all U.S. adults parallel the like trends among college alumni.

B. Studies of College Professors

The average American college professor has had more years of formal education than the average college alumnus or adult. Therefore, a comparison of the religious faith of professors with that of the average alumnus or adult should help to show the effect of formal education on such faith. I have found six relevant scientific studies. So far as I am aware, the only previous review of this literature is the one-paragraph 1976 review by Hoge and Keeter noted later.

I also review here one study of elementary and high school teachers.

1. Leuba, 1914

In 1914 James H. Leuba, professor of psychology at Bryn Mawr and the great pioneer in scientific research on religious faith, sent religious question- naires to about one-fifth of the physical and bio- logical scientists listed in Cattell's American Men of Science (1910), and received replies from 75% of them. About 60% of these scientists were college professors.

In his questionnaire he asked about belief in a personal God who answers prayers, and about belief in personal immortality. He found that only 40% of his pollees claimed to believe in such a God, and only 49% in personal immortality (Leuba, 1950: 35). These figures are far below any later national figures for college alumni or for the American people, which implies that in 1914 American professors of physical and biological science were far less religious than the average alumnus or American adult.

In 1914 Leuba also queried more than half of the professors listed as members of the American Historical Association, omitting the few professors in Roman Catholic institutions, and found that only 45% claimed to believe in a personal deity, and only 52% in personal immortality (ibid: 37).

He used the 1913 membership list of the American Sociological Society to question one-third (197) of its members, excluding only professors in Catholic schools. He divided his respondents into two clas- ses, professors and nonprofessors. He found that 55% of the nonprofessors claimed to believe in a personal God, and 61% in personal immortality. These figures are far above his corresponding figures for professors of sociology, namely 24% and 40% (ibid: 38).

Using the 1914 membership list of the American Psychological Association, Leuba polled about 100 professors of psychology, and found that only 24% believed in a personal God, and only 20% in personal immortality (ibid: 39).

In 1933 Leuba replicated his polls of physical scientists, biologists, sociologists, and psycholo- gists—most of whom were professors—and found that nearly all percentages of belief had declined sharply. Overall, belief in a personal God fell from 42% to 30%, and belief in personal immortality from 51 to 33% (ibid: 47). These declines were probably much greater than those for the general adult population.

It is surely remarkable that Leuba's research was never replicated by other investigators, who in fact made no studies of the religiosity of college professors for the next thirty years.

2. M. H. Harper, 1927

In 1922 Manly H. Harper (TC, Columbia) gave an agreement-disagreement test on social beliefs and attitudes to more than 2900 educators scattered throughout the U.S. (elementary teachers 60%, high school 24%). The test included 71 propositions. Of the first 21 propositions, five concerned religious faith. The chief purpose of the test was to distinguish between liberals and conservatives.

The answers enabled Harper to segregate an "exceptionally non-conservative group" and a "representatively conservative group of educators." He found that there was a strong correlation between liberalism in religious beliefs and liberalism in social beliefs and attitudes.

He determined the number of years of education of each educator and correlated these numbers with their overall liberalism scores. He found a correlation of +.521 + .032, which strongly suggests that each additional year of education makes men more liberal in religious belief, as well as in most social beliefs and attitudes (Harper, 1927: 67).

3. Thalheimer, 1965, 1973

After Leuba the next researcher to study the religious beliefs of U.S. college professors was Fred Thalheimer of San Francisco State College. In 1961 he mailed a 15-page questionnaire to all the faculty members (about 1400) of a large West Coast state university, and obtained 741 usable replies. Most of his questions were about church affiliation, attendance, and prayer, but he asked several questions about belief in God. He found that only 38% believed in a God who "may be appealed to personally," that 20% were atheists, and 28% were agnostics (Thalheimer, 1965: 102, 106). These percentages differ radically from those for all college alumni, or for the general U.S. population, and prove that in 1961 these professors were far less religious than the typical American.

In 1973 Thalheimer reported additional conclusions based on his 1961 study. He noted that his
conclusion on low religiosity among academicians "is
substantially unchanged" when applied to "persons
educationally and occupationally most similar to
academicians" (Thalheimer, 1973: 184).

4. Glenn and Weiner, 1967

In 1967 Norval D. Glenn and David Weiner mailed
questionnaires to 760 active members of the American
Sociological Association, including a question on
current "religious preference." They found that
35.7% of their pollees claimed to have no "religious
preference," a figure about 16 times that for all
U.S. adults (2.1%) in 1957 (Glenn and Weiner, 1969:
297). Of course, "no religious preference" does not
mean no religious faith, but it suggests far less
religious faith on the average than any statement of
religious preference.

5. Steinberg

In his book, The Academic Melting Pot (1974),
Stephen Steinberg analyzed in detail the religious
data collected by a Carnegie-American Council on
Education 1969 survey of some 400,000 American
college faculty members. He reported that 22% of
them claimed to have no "current religious affiliation." Religious affiliation is a far broader term
than church membership. It includes persons who have
religious preferences, as well as those who are
church members. According to Steinberg, this 22%
"far exceeds the level of nonaffiliation in the
general population," which was then "approximately
5%" (p. 136).
The Carnegie-ACE poll also allowed pollees to
classify themselves into four classes by degree and
amount of faith, and reported the following results:
"deeply religious," 16%; "moderately religious," 48%;
"indifferent to religion," 28%; and "opposed to
religion," 8% (p. 135).
For comparison, a 1976 Gallup poll classified
U.S. adult males into four similar classes, and found
that 66% claimed that religion was "very important"
to them, a figure far higher than the 16% of faculty
members who claimed to be "deeply religious." The
Gallup poll reported that only 5% claimed that religion is "not at all important," and only 8% "not too
important," far less than the 36% of faculty members

-68-

who claimed to be "opposed to religion," 8%, or "indifferent to religion," 28% (G. H. Gallup, 1978: 624).

6. Caplovitz and Sherrow, 1977

In 1977 David Caplovitz and Fred Sherrow further analyzed the Carnegie-ACE 1969 survey data, and reported that "Faculty rates of Apostasy...in 1969 are, in each religion, substantially higher than those of college seniors in 1961. Thus...among Protestant professors 24% were apostates," compared with 12% for Protestant seniors in 1961-64, and among Catholic professors the rate was also 24% compared with only 7% among Catholic seniors in 1961-64 (Caplovitz and Sherrow, 1977: 85).

Caplovitz and Sherrow also found that the faculty apostasy rate varied radically, continuously, and directly with the quality of the school where they taught. The rates were 18% in "low" quality schools for both Protestant and Catholic professors, and 34% in "high" quality schools for both groups of professors. For "medium" quality schools the rate was 23%. The authors noted that another survey had revealed that at Columbia University, "one of the great universities," the apostasy rates were much higher, 60% for Protestant professors, and 50% for Catholics (Ibid: 86-87). Professors in such prestigious schools are not only the best educated and the most intellectually gifted, but also feel more free to express their rejection of religious dogma.

7. Hoge and Keeter, 1976

In 1976 Dean R. Hoge of Catholic University and Larry G. Keeter of Appalachian State University published an article on "Determinants of College Teachers' Religious Beliefs and Participation." In a preliminary one-paragraph review of the literature (Hoge and Keeter, 1976: 221) they asserted that "Past research on religion of college teachers agrees" that they "are less traditionally religious...than the general population (Lehman and Witty, 1931; Leuba, 1950; Stark, 1963; Thalheimer, 1965; Wilensky and Ladinsky, 1967; Anderson, 1968; DeJong and Faulkner, 1972; Steinberg, 1974)." I have not reviewed all of these studies because two seem to be irrelevant or unclear, and one (DeJong) was unavailable.

8. Comments

All of the 14 polls of college professors reviewed or noted above support the conclusion that professors are much less religious in belief than either other adults or college alumni. Since most college professors have had one or more years of graduate education, these studies provide additional support for the general conclusion that every additional year of higher education is associated with, and probably a partial cause of, a decrease in religious faith. Moreover, as professors are on average about 20 years older than their students, these studies also strongly suggest again that the antireligious effect of higher education is not temporary.

C. The Effect of Education on U.S. Adult Faith

Having completed my survey of the relevant data obtained from scientific polling of U.S. students and professors, I turn now to survey the relevant data obtained by polling samples of the U.S. adult population. I believe that this is the first review of such data ever published.

The great majority of the student polls reviewed above were conducted before 1970. The great majority of the adult polls reviewed below were conducted after 1970.

1. Catholic Digest Poll, 1952, 1965

In both 1952 and 1965 the Catholic Digest employed professional pollers (Ben Gaffin and Associates) to conduct similar nation-wide adult religious polls, and the respondents were classified into five classes by amount of education (0-8 years, 9-11 years, 12 years, 13-15 years, and college graduate). On all questions concerning belief in basic Christian dogmas, both the 1952 and the 1965 polls revealed that belief varied markedly and inversely with amount of formal education. For instance, the 1965 poll revealed that 87% of the grade school group claimed to "believe in a God" and that the percent fell steadily for each of four better educated groups (85, 82, 78, 66), reaching a low of 66% for college graduates (Marty et al, 1968: 216).

The 1965 percent of those who "believe Jesus Christ was God" also fell almost steadily—78, 79, 73, 67, 55—from the grade school to the college graduate group (ibid: 224).

For belief in "heaven," the 1965 percent fell steadily--74, 72, 68, 67, 51--as the amount of education rose (ibid: 248). For belief in "hell" the percentages fell even faster--65, 61, 52, 47, 38 (ibid: 250).

2. Ford Appalachian Survey, 1960

In the late 1950s the University of North Carolina Survey Operations Unit surveyed 1466 Southern Appalachian households in a study of social change. In 1960 Thomas R. Ford of the University of Kentucky published an analysis of some of the data on religious beliefs collected in that survey. He reported that belief in two basic Christian doctrines varied inversely with amount of education. Belief that "God will reward some people and punish others after death" fell from 73.6% for 288 persons with up to 6 years of education to 66.2% for 590 persons with 12 or more years of education. Belief that "The Bible is God's word and all it says is true" fell from 80% for those with six years or less of education to 44% for 300 college alumni (Ford, 1960: 45).

3. Glenn and Hyland, 1967

In 1966 Norval D. Glenn and Ruth Hyland, both of the University of Texas, analyzed the data on social status, education, and religious preference collected in four Gallup national polls (November, 1963, to March, 1965). They found that these polls revealed that white pollees who expressed no religious preference were better educated than those who reported a religious preference. For instance, 23.2% of those who had no religious preference were college graduates, but only 9.2% of all pollees were college graduates (Glenn and Hyland, 1967: 79). Since persons with no religious preference are less religious in faith than other persons, these data imply that amount of education varies inversely with amount of religious faith.

4. Stan Gaede, 1977

In or about 1975, J. H. Kauffman and L. Harder studied the social and religious traits of 3591 U.S. Mennonites. In 1976, sociologist Stan Gaede of Gordon College carried out a secondary analysis of their data on 1818 male nonstudents. He reported

(Gaede, 1977: 249), an inverse correlation of -.27 between education (measured by the years of formal schooling) and religious belief orthodoxy (measured by the addition of scores on a Glock-Stark scale and a Kauffman-Harder scale).

5. Roof, North Carolina, 1978

In or about 1976 the North Carolina Diocese of the Episcopalian Church asked Wade Clark Roof to poll a random sample of its lay members on their religiosity, education, and other traits. He queried 890 adult members, received 518 replies, and used 486 replies from white subjects. He reported a negative correlation of -.23, between degree of religious belief orthodoxy and amount of formal education, and a positive correlation of .24 between belief orthodoxy and church attendance (Roof, 1978: 122).

6. The Caplow Middletown Poll, 1978

In 1978, Caplow, Bahr, Chadwick et al polled 220 adults in Muncie, Indiana (the Lynd's Middletown) on the "frequency of private prayer," and classified the pollees by amount of education. They reported that the percent of those who "never pray" rose from 10% for those with no college education, to 12% for "some college, to 16% for "college graduates," and to 21 for pollees with an "advanced degree" (Caplow et al, 1983: 327). While prayer is religious behavior, not belief, it is firm evidence of belief in a personal god, one who answers prayer. People who "never pray" obviously do not believe in such a God.

7. Gallup Polls on Individual Religious Beliefs

Over the past forty years the well-known Gallup organization (American Institute of Public Opinion) has often polled a representative sample of U.S. adults on their religious opinions. Unfortunately, it has made little effort to ask the most significant questions, or to ask the same question at regular intervals, so as to facilitate scientific determination of long-run trends. And it has often failed to classify pollees by the amount of their education. The Gallup Poll is a profit-seeking firm, not a research institute. Nevertheless, it deserves special praise for collecting more data on trends in U.S. adult religious opinion, and on the relation of

education to adult religious faith, than any research institute. Nearly all of its relevant polls
have shown that the most educated adults are the
least religious.

(1) On Belief in God

For instance, a 1954 poll of U.S. adults revealed that belief "in God," unqualified, fell from
97% for those with grade school education or less, to
96% for those with some high school education, and
to 92% for college alumni. The combined figures for
agnostics ("undecided") and atheists are more significant. The totals for these two classes rose from
3 to 4 to 8%, with increased education. In this
poll, as in all pre-1971 Gallup polls, belief in
God included belief in an impersonal spirit or
natural force, which explains the high percentage of
believers (G. H. Gallup, 1972: 1293).

In 1975 Gallup polled U.S. adults on a very
similar question, belief in a God or universal spirit,
undescribed, and reported almost the same decline in
belief with increased education: 96%, 96%, 91% (G. H.
Gallup, 1978: 627).

In 1975 Gallup also asked about belief in a God
or spirit who "observes your actions and rewards or
punishes you for them," a basic orthodox religious
belief far more significant than mere belief in an
undescribed God or spirit. The answers revealed
that only 56% of college alumni who believed in a
God or Spirit (91%) also believed in an observing,
rewarding, and punishing God or spirit. Thus only
51% of all college alumni accepted the latter idea.
The net belief figures for the high school group was
73%; for the grade school group 76% (ibid: 628).

(2). On Belief in an Afterlife

In June, 1968, Gallup polled U.S. adults on
several beliefs about the afterlife, and classified
the respondents into three groups based on education. The answers revealed that belief in heaven
among 950 Protestants declined from 96% for those
with 0-8 years of education to 91% for those with
9-12 years, and to 79% for college alumni. For 344
Catholics, the like figures were 85%, 91%, and 79%.
Protestant belief in hell declined from 77%, to 69%,
to 56% with more education. The percent of Protestant belief in life after death actually rose with
more education—77, 78, 79—but these data are very

suspect because they show that 19% of grade-school
Protestant believers in heaven (96%) did not believe
in life after death (Alston, 1972: 181).

In 1975 Gallup again polled U.S. adults on their
belief in life after death. He reported that such
belief fell from 75% for his grade school group, to
70% for his high school group, and to 66% for college
alumni (G. H. Gallup, 1978: 628). Unfortunately, he
did not report figures for college graduates, or for
persons with advanced degrees, which would almost
certainly have revealed further declines in belief.

In spite of these findings, George Gallup, Jr.
claimed in 1982 that "Gallup found that college-
educated Americans are more likely to hold such a
belief in an afterlife than those with a high school
education or less" (G. Gallup, Jr., 1982: 47). He
cited a 1982 poll, but gave no figures. I have been
unable to find a more detailed version of this poll.

(3). On Belief in Divinity of Christ

The dogma that Jesus Christ is divine, i.e.,
more than human, is a basic Christian doctrine. In
1981 Gallup polled U.S. adults on their opinion of
this doctrine, permitting only five answers: "completely true, mostly true, no opinion, mostly untrue,"
and "completely untrue." The results revealed that
acceptance of this dogma varied inversely and strongly
with amount of education. For instance, 19% of college
alumni rated the doctrine as "completely" or "mostly
untrue," while only 6% of those with some high school
education, and 3% of those with less education, did
so. The percent who rated it "completely true" rose
from 48% for college alumni, to 61% for some high
school education, to 74% for those with less education
(G. H. Gallup, 1982: 122). No separate figures for
college graduates were given.

(4). On Belief in Creationism

The doctrine that God created man and all other
animals in their present form was long an almost
universally accepted basic Christian dogma. In 1982
Gallup surveyed U.S. adults on their belief in this
dogma, creationism, in evolution with God, and in
evolution without God. The survey revealed that
acceptance of creationism varied inversely and strongly
with amount of education. The degree of acceptance
rose from 24% among college graduates, to 36% among
other college alumni, to 49% among the high school

group, and to 52% among the grade school or less group. Conversely, belief in evolution without God fell from 17% among college graduates, to 12%, to 7%, and to 5% respectively (G. H. Gallup, 1983a: 208-09).

In 1981 Mervin D. Field, a professional poller, polled Californians on their belief in creationism and evolution. He too found that belief in creationism varied greatly and inversely with amount of education, ranging from 63% for those with no college education, to 50% for those with some college education, and to 25% for college graduates (Field, 1981: 9). He offered no figures for those with graduate degrees.

(5). Belief in Prayer and the Bible

Another 1981 Gallup poll asked U.S. adults to evaluate (with five choices) the statement, "I constantly seek God's will through prayer." The results revealed that 45% of college alumni rated it as "completely" or "mostly untrue," while only 26% of adults with some high school education only, and a mere 11% of those with less education, did so. Conversely, the figures for complete acceptance of this statement rose from 19% for the college alumni, to 25% for the high school group, and to 45% for the grade school group (G. H. Gallup, 1982b: 114).

In 1981 Gallup also polled U.S. adults on their opinion of the Christian Bible. The poll revealed that only 21% of college alumni considered it the "literal word of God," while 40% of the high school group, and 56% of the grade school group, did so. Conversely, belief that the Bible is a "book of fables" fell from 22% for the college group, to 7%, and to 2% (G. H. Gallup, 1982a: 174).

Similar Gallup polls on the Bible in 1976 and 1980 had yielded similar results (G. H. Gallup, 1978: 861; and 1981: 187).

(6). Belief in Suicide and Abortion

In 1975 Gallup polled U.S. adults on their stand towards suicide by the incurably ill. Such suicide has long been condemned by Christian theologians and priests. He reported that 54% of college alumni approved of such suicide, compared with 38% for his high school group, and only 23% for his grade school group (G. H. Gallup, 1978: 462).

There has long been strong opposition to abortion among conservative Christian theologians. The Pope has repeatedly denounced it. Therefore, the fact that support of abortion varies directly with amount of education provides further evidence that religious faith is reduced by education.

In 1974, 1975, 1981, and 1983 Gallup polled U.S. adults on their attitude towards the Supreme Court decision legalizing abortion, or towards abortion "when wanted." All four polls revealed that support for legal abortion varied directly and greatly with amount of education.

For instance, in 1983 only 35% of U.S. college alumni condemned the 1973 Supreme Court decision legalizing abortion, while the figure rose to 44% for the high school group, and to 54% for the grade school group. The figures for approval of the decision were 60, 49, and 36%, in the same order (G. H. Gallup, 1983b: 17). The positive correlations between amount of education and approval of abortion had been still higher in 1974 (G. H. Gallup, 1978: 249), in 1975 (ibid: 492), and in 1981 (G. H. Gallup, 1982a: 112).

(7)   Other Religious Beliefs

In 1957, 1974, and 1981 Gallup polled Americans on their belief that "religion can answer problems." In both 1974 and 1981 (but not in 1957) the percent who believed so was far higher among those with only a grade school education (73% both years) than among those with some college education (52 and 57%). The corresponding rates for the high school group were 63 and 67% (G. H. Gallup, 1982a: 61).

In 1981 Gallup also polled Americans on the importance of "following God's will," and allowed pollees to grade the importance from 0 to 10. Of respondents with only some grade school education, 66% gave the highest score, 10, to this importance, while only 39% of college alumni did so. Moreover, 7% of the college alumni gave it a zero score, while only 1% of the grade school group did so (Gallup Poll, 1982a: 13).

In 1983 Gallup polled Americans on their support for a constitutional amendment permitting voluntary prayer in public schools. He found that 81% of the general public, but only 72% of college alumni, supported this amendment. For his grade school group the percent of approval was a high 94% (San Francisco Chronicle, 9-8-83, p. 24).

8.   Comments on Adult Polls

It is remarkable and very significant that nearly all of the 29 adult polls reviewed above reveal a marked inverse correlation between amount of formal education and amount of religious faith. Except for two polls on belief in an afterlife, I have not been able to find a professional poll of adults which supports a different conclusion.

The revealed negative correlation among American adults is much greater than that normally found among college students because the differences in amount of education are much greater among all adults than among college students.

The general conclusion that there is a marked negative correlation between amount of formal education and amount of religious faith in the entire U.S. adult population includes and rests upon several more limited and specific conclusions, each of which is supported by one or more, usually several, of the adult surveys reviewed above.

1.   Adults with some high school education are less religious in faith than are their age peers with no high school education.

2.   College alumni are less religious in faith than are their age peers with no college education.

3.   College graduates are less religious in faith than are their contemporary college alumni.

Since all of these conclusions, general and specific, apply to the entire U.S. adult population, they prove that the effect of secondary and higher education on amount of religious faith is not temporary, but continues throughout the lives of educated persons.

D.   Aging and Religious Faith

There has been a vast expansion of both secondary and higher education in the U.S. during this century. As a result there is now a strong inverse correlation between age and amount of such education. If every additional year of such education tends to make people less religious, the amount of religious faith should vary directly with age at any given time. Many studies and polls have shown that this positive correlation exists from age 30 on (Argyle, 1958: 67-69). This correlation provides further evidence that every increase in the amount of formal secondary and higher education is associated with a reduction in religious faith.

E.   Sex and Religious Faith

Until recently, American girls received much less higher education than boys. In 1970 only 8.6% of white females over age 24 had completed four years of

-77-

college, while the male figure was 15.0% (<u>Statistical</u>
<u>Abstract of the U.S., 1972</u>: 112).

Many studies including all relevant Gallup polls,
have revealed that women are less religious in faith
than men. For instance, a 1981 Gallup poll reported
that 40% of U.S. females, and only 34% of males,
believed that the Bible "is the actual word of God,
and is to be taken literally, word for word" (G. H.
Gallup, 1982b: 174).

These two facts, that women have less education
and that they are more religious in faith, clearly
suggest that there is a negative correlation between
amount of education and amount of religious faith.

In his discussion of sex differences in religious
behavior and faith, Argyle noted two possible reasons—
greater female guilt feelings, and greater attraction
to a male deity—but he ignored the important effect
of differences in amount of education (Argyle, 1958:
78-79).

F.   Race and Religious Faith

Several Gallup Polls on religious faith have
classified pollees by race, white or nonwhite. All
such polls have revealed that whites are less religious than nonwhites. For instance, a 1980 poll on
the Bible found that only 37% of whites believed the
Bible to be the "actual word of God," while the figure
for nonwhites was 56% (G. H. Gallup, 1981: 187). It
is well-known that, on average, nonwhites, who are
mostly negroes, have had less formal education than
whites. These two facts suggest again that the amount
of religious faith varies inversely with the length of
formal education.

G.   General Conclusions

It is very significant that all but 2 of the over
50 student opinion polls, all 14 of the faculty polls,
all but 2 of the 29 general adult opinion polls, and
all studies of age, sex, and race differences reviewed
in this chapter support part or all of the same general
conclusion, namely that there is a significant, and in
most cases marked, negative correlation between amount
of secondary and higher education and amount of religious faith in the U.S. This negative correlation
strongly implies that every increase in the number of
years of such education tends to make people less
religious.

Although it is almost certain that, other factors being equal, every additional year of secondary and higher education tends, on average, to make students and adults less religious in the amount and/or the intensity of their religious belief, there is another major factor which is partially responsible for the negative correlation between amount of higher education and amount of faith, namely differences in native intelligence. The most intelligent people tend to stay in school longer than the less intelligent. Each school year some students, usually the less intelligent, drop out of school. Numerous studies have revealed that the less intelligent are more religious than other people (Argyle, 1958: 93). Therefore, college graduates are both more intelligent and better educated than other adults, and both facts help to explain why they are much less religious than other persons.

H. Explanation

Having reviewed the data which support the conclusion that, on average, every additional year of secondary and higher education reduces religious faith, I turn now to suggest some reasons why such education has this effect.

First, secondary and higher education expose most young people for the first time to plausible arguments against some or all religious dogmas. Most American youths have been protected from antireligious speakers and writers, and are first exposed to their ideas in high school or college. In college they also learn of gifted and famous agnostics and atheists.

Secondly, few American young people learn much about science and the scientific method of reasoning until they enter high school or college. And every additional course in science tends to weaken faith in one or more religious dogmas. Education teaches most people to think more clearly and reason more logically, as the best scientists do.

Thirdly, the study of history in high school and college trends to weaken religious faith because it reveals how many different religious doctrines have waxed and waned in the past, and how many different, conflicting religions are still widely accepted in other countries. This naturally causes some students to ask how conflicts between religious claims can be settled. Theologians have no answer for this question, and realization of this fact creates religious doubt.

Fourth, educated adults are more successful in life than other people. This tends to make them more self-confident and independent than other persons. As a result, they feel less need for supernatural aid and comfort than other people do. They learn to rely less on prayer, and more on personal effort, to achieve personal goals.

Fifth, since college professors are both much more intelligent and much better educated than other Americans, they tend to be much less religious, and students are influenced by their professors. The most able professors teach the most advanced courses, so that every additional year of college education exposes students to more criticism of orthodox religious dogmas like creationism.

Sixth, graduate students flock to elite universitues, whose most eminent professors are markedly less religious than their less eminent colleagues in less prestigious universities. When the most gifted and most highly educated Ph.Ds. from elite universities become college professors, they naturally spread the attitudes they acquired or strengthened as graduate students.

Seventh, in some industries and professions, educated specialists must learn to accept and use antireligious scientific theories in order to be successful in their profession, or in order to earn higher wages and profits. For instance, oil geologists must use the anti-religious theories of geological and biological evolution in order to find oil deposits. Biologists and plant breeders must use the theory of biological evolution to breed improved animals and plants. Medical researchers must ignore or reject belief in miracles and in seizure by devils and evil spirits in order to determine the effects of new drugs and medical treatments.

Finally, every additional year of higher education must surely make it more difficult to believe in and respect a superior being who sends sinners and unbaptized children to hell, and who insists upon constant praise and worship.

At the end of the next chapter I shall offer reasons why religious faith varies inversely with native intelligence. Some of these reasons help to explain the effects of higher education, as well as those of higher intelligence.

I turn now to try to explain another important conclusion, namely that most loss of student religious faith, from 1914 to 1983, probably occurred before students entered college. The kind of students who go on to college, especially those who enter elite schools, have IQs 15-25 points higher on average than those who do not. As shown in the following chapter, the amount of a person's religious faith varies inversely with his or her IQ. The more intelligent students are, on average, the first to lose some or all of their religious faith, and usually do so before entering college.

Moreover, most of the best high school students have parents who have had some college education, and the children of such more intelligent parents acquire less religious faith, and lose it more quickly.

CHAPTER III

THE EFFECT OF INTELLIGENCE ON U.S. RELIGIOUS FAITH

In the long war between religion and science, religionists have often asserted or implied that religious believers are more intelligent than non-believers, and the latter have often asserted or implied the opposite, but, until the invention and wide use of scientific intelligence tests and public opinion polls, there was no scientific method of settling this dispute. Since 1900 a growing mass of scientific data relevant to this dispute has been produced, but I have been unable to find any summary of this data, or indeed any book, essay, chapter, or article on the effect of intelligence on religious faith and/or behavior. I believe that this essay may be the first ever written on this subject, and, in any case, by far the most comprehensive.

Although American intelligence testers have tested very large numbers of people each year for over 80 years, and although researchers have repeatedly correlated intelligence test scores with race, sex, occupation, age, political opinion, psychological traits, etc., relatively little research on the correlation between IQ scores and religious faith or behavior has been done, and the results of such research have been virtually ignored by both religionist and writers on intelligence tests. For instance, the 1040 page Handbook of Human Intelligence (1982), edited by Robert Sternberg, contains no reference to religion in its index or table of contents.

There is an extensive literature on the relationship between amount of formal education and amount of religious faith or behavior. But the question of whether religious faith varies with native intelligence is quite distinct from the question of whether it varies with amount of education.

In his authoritative book, Religious Behavior (1958), Michael Argyle devoted two pages to a brief summary of the conclusions of six pioneer quantitative studies of the relationship of intelligence to religious faith among U.S. students (Argyle, 1958: 92-93). In 1975 Norman G. Poythress, in a single paragraph, listed and summarized the findings of nine studies of the relationship between religiosity (defined to include religious behavior as well as faith) and intelligence (Poythress, 1975: 272). Poythress failed to mention Argyle's summary, and ignored five of the six studies summarized by Argyle. In this essay I review all of the relevant published studies cited by Argyle and Poythress, and over 30 polls not mentioned by either of them.

There are several possible reasons for the long neglect of this intelligence-faith relationship, a subject of wide and often intense interest. First, some men suspect that intelligence tests do not measure native intelligence. But this suspicion has not prevented the publication of many books and articles on the relationship of intelligence to race, sex, occupation, age, etc. Secondly, there is the suspicion that we cannot measure religious faith, but this suspicion has not prevented the conduct of many statistical studies on the growth or decline of religious faith. The only plausible remaining reason is that researchers know or suspect that a comprehensive review of the relevant data will yield a very unpopular conclusion, namely that nonreligious persons are more intelligent than religious persons.

In order to determine the correlation between native intelligence and religious faith, one must measure both intelligence and faith. Several well-known, long-used intelligence tests are available, but no such widely accepted measure of religious faith is available. For this reason, researchers on intelligence and religiosity have used many different and imperfect measures of religious faith. Most have used questions concerning belief in one or two religious dogmas, such as belief in a personal God. When such a single aspect of religious faith is used, only very crude relationships between intelligence and faith can be determined. But the fact that they are crude does not mean that they are insignificant or irrelevant.

To permit differentiation among those who believe in one or more religious dogmas, some researchers have allowed respondents to indicate the degree of their belief or disbelief. This allows a more complete and accurate determination of the degree of correlation between intelligence and religiosity.

Other researchers have achieved a greater differentiation by using a series of questions about different religious dogmas. Ideally, both methods should be used. It would also be desirable to weight answers, because belief in certain basic religious dogmas, those of so-called natural religion, is more significant than belief in minor or sectarian religious dogmas.

My primary purpose in this chapter is to survey studies on the correlation between intelligence and religious faith, but I report some studies of the relationship of intelligence to measures of religiosit which include religious behavior or which measure religious behavior only. I do so because there is a high correlation between religious faith and religious behavior.

This survey of the scientific, quantitative literature on the relationship of native intelligence to Christian religious faith in the U.S. is divided into six main parts: (1) a review of studies of the correlation between individual student intelligence test scores and individual religious-faith test scores (2) a review of relevant student-body comparisons, (3) a note on my earlier review of the religious faith scores of college professors, (4) a review of the religiosity scores of geniuses, (5) a review of the religiosity scores of highly successful persons, and (6) a note on my previous review of relevant Gallup polls. I also comment briefly on the literature on th effects of education and aging on religious faith.

A.   Individual Student Intelligence and Religious Faith

The best way to determine the correlation between intelligence and religious faith is to give individual intelligence and religious-faith tests to representative samples of the general adult population. So far as I am aware, this has never been done. However, researchers have obtained and compared the results of individual intelligence and religiosity tests of at least 21 groups of students, using a variety of differ ent intelligence and faith tests. In this section I review all such studies known to me.

1.   T. H. Howells, 1928

So far as I am aware, the first scientist to explicitly investigate the correlation between native intelligence and amount of religious faith was Thomas H. Howells, a professor of psychology at the Universit of Iowa. In April, 1926, he tested 461 students in elementary psychology classes on their acceptance or rejection of twelve religious statements (ten items of faith, one on respect for preachers, and one on enjoyment of sermons). He then used available composite scores on the Thorndike Intelligence Test, Part I, anc on the Iowa Comprehension Test to correlate religiosit

with intelligence. He reported a negative coefficient
of correlation of -.36 $\pm$ .026, which means that the
degree of religiosity varied inversely and substantially with intelligence.

Howells segregated the 36 religiously most "radical" students and the 34 religiously most conservative
students, and determined the mean percentile composite
intelligence score for each group. He reported a
mean intelligence score of 72.8 for the radicals, and
44.5 for the conservatives, the difference being 6.14
times the probable error (Howells, 1928: 47).

He also used   other available data on the intelligence of his students—college grade points, college
entrance tests, his own "test of rational judgement,"
maze problem scores, and other test results—to determine their correlation with his religiosity scores.
He reported that "in all the tests of intellectual
ability the typical conservative always made the poorer
score...that in most of the tests the differences are
large enough practically to guarantee" that they are
significant, and that "the different bits of supporting
evidence are mutually supporting" and "constitute
fairly convincing evidence that" the religiously conservative students "are, in general, relatively
inferior in intellectual ability."

Howells failed to note that his findings were
implicit in Leuba's earlier conclusions concerning the
religious faith of eminent scientists. In turn, his
findings were ignored by most later researchers.

It is noteworthy that, although Howells was the
first to investigate the correlation between individual
intelligence and religiosity, his study was more
thorough and better designed than that of any subsequent researcher. For instance, he used 12 different
religious questions and 10 different tests of native
intelligence, and tested 461 students. He was a
brilliant pioneer in the study of the relationship of
intelligence to religiosity. Nearly all later researchers confirmed his conclusions that intelligence
varies inversely with the amount of religious faith.

2. Sinclair, 1928

In his book, Religious Behavior (1958), Michael
Argyle briefly summarized a 1928 study by R. D.
Sinclair, "A Comparative Study of those who Report
the Experience of the Divine Presence and those Who Do
Not" (p. 93). According to Argyle, Sinclair tested
500 students and reported a negative correlation of
-.27 between such religious experience and IQ. I have

been unable to obtain a copy of Sinclair's article. Experiencing a divine presence is different from holding a religious belief, but it implies a strong belief in the existence of a God.

3. H. B. Carlson, 1934

The next scientific study of the correlation between individual intelligence and religious faith was conducted by Hilding B. Carlson among seniors at the University of Chicago in 1931-32. He used the Thurston-Chave Reality of God Test (scale 22, A) to measure religious faith, and compared the results with intelligence test scores. Only 215 of the 500 seniors returned completed forms, which may have biased the results. He reported an inverse correlation ($-.191 + .059$) between a favorable or conservative attitude towards God, on the one hand, and intelligence, on the other. In his words, "there is a tendency for the more intelligent undergraduate to be sympathetic toward...atheism," and this conclusion "coincides with the conclusions of most other investigators," whom he did not name (Carlson, 1934: 208).

Carlson also used the Thurstone test on attitude toward birth control, and this enabled him to determine a positive correlation of $.211 + .064$ between approval of birth control and intelligence test scores Since disapproval of birth control is a dogma of the Catholic Church and many Protestant sects, this correlation supports the conclusion that the amount of religious faith varies inversely with intelligence.

4. Franzblau, 1934

Professor Abraham N.Franzblau of Hebrew Union College gave a Terman intelligence test and a religious belief test to 354 Jewish children age 10-16, and reported an inverse correlation of $-.15$ between his religious and intelligence test scores. He also gave a Terman mental age test, and found an inverse correlation of $-.35$ between these scores and the religious test scores (Franzblau, 1934: 38).

Franzblau summarized the results of the previous studies by Howells and Sinclair, and asserted that his results "apparently confirm their findings."

5. Corey, 1940

In 1934 Stephen M. Corey (Un. of Wisconsin) polle 234 female UW freshmen on their "attitude toward God,"

using a Thurstone-Chave attitude scale (form unspeci-
fied). He had access to their scores on the Ohio
State Psychological Examination (form 17). He reported a positive correlation of + .10 + .04 between
the intelligence test scores and the "attitude toward
God" test scores (Corey, 1940: 345). He claimed that
his results disagreed with those obtained by Carlson,
but did not try to explain this conflict. The chief
reason for this conflict may be that he used a different, less relevant, religiosity test, and gave it
only to females, who are more studious and religious
than males.

Corey also reported a positive correlation
(+ .15 + .04) between a favorable attitude towards
the theory of evolution and intelligence scores. This
supports Carlson's finding of a negative correlation
between religious faith and intelligence, but Corey
did not make this point.

6. T. A. Symington, 1935

In 1935 Thomas A. Symington published a monograph,
Religious Liberals and Conservatives, in which he
reported on a recent scientific study of, among other
things, the correlation between intelligence and
religious faith. He used a Y.M.C.A. "Test of Religious
Thinking" consisting of 100 questions in nine groups,
most but not all of which involved belief in religious
doctrines, to determine the degree of religious liberalism of some 400 young people in several colleges and
church groups. He then gave all of them either an
Otis or a Thurstone Test of Mental Ability—he claimed
they were very similar—and determined the correlations
between intelligence and religious scores separately
for six different groups—three for respondents with a
conservative background and three for those with a
liberal background. He reported that, "There is a
constant positive relation in all the groups between
liberal religious thinking and mental ability, but the
correlations are much larger in the groups from a
liberal background [average + .46] than in the groups
from a conservative background" [average + .23].
He added that, "There is also a constant positive
relation between liberal scores and intelligence in
each of the nine parts of the Test of Religious Thinking," including all five parts devoted to questions of
doctrinal faith (Symington, 1935: 40, 98).

7. Vernon Jones, 1938

During the years 1930-35 Vernon Jones, of Clark University, gave three religious tests and an intelligence test to 381 students, including all freshmen in four class years. He used Thurstone-Chave tests on attitude toward God (influence on conduct), on the reality of God, and on attitude towards the Church. All students were given the American Council Psychological Examination, which measured scholastic aptitude or intelligence.

Jones concluded that there was "a slight tendency for high intelligence and liberal attitudes to go together." He reported positive correlations of +.20 (conduct), +.28 (reality), and +.23 (church) between intelligence and liberal religious scores for 268 freshmen. For 100 seniors the correlations were +.20, +.11, and +.23. He claimed that all these correlations were "reliable statistically" (Jones, 1938: 114-15, 132).

8. Gilliland, 1940

In 1940 psychologist A. R. Gilliland published a report of his study of Northwestern students. He gave three Thurstone-Chave Attitude toward God tests (forms A, B, and C) to 339 students, and compared the results with the students' intelligence test scores. He reported that he had found "little or no relationship between intelligence and attitude toward God" (Gilliland, 1940: 15).

He noted that his results differed from those obtained by Carlson, and suggested that the difference might be due to the fact that Carlson had used "only students who returned blanks," while he had obtained returns from all his pollees. He ignored the results obtained by Howells, Sinclair, Franzblau, and Symmington, all of whom had confirmed Carlson's conclusion.

As explained below, nearly all later studies also confirmed Carlson's finding of a negative correlation. It therefore seems probable that Gilliland's sample of students was abnormal or that his research methodology was faulty. He used three Attitude to God tests while Carlson had used only one, more relevant, "reality of God" test (22, A). It is noteworthy that Gilliland's conclusions on sex differences in faith and on the effect of education on faith were also very abnormal.

9. Gragg, 1942

In 1942 Donald B. Gragg of Hardin-Simmons University published a report of his study of the "religious
attitudes" of 438 students in three small denominational colleges in the southwestern part of the "Bible
Belt." He used the Thurstone - Chave Reality of God
(22, A) and also obtained American Council on Education (ACE) psychological test scores for 100 freshmen
at one college. He reported an inverse correlation
(-.13 + .07) between ACE intelligence scores and the
"reality of God" scores for these 100 freshmen (Gragg,
1942, 245, 251).

10. Brown and Lowe, 1951

In their 1948 study of 613 male and female liberal
arts students at the University of Denver, D. G.
Brown and W. L. Lowe determined and segregated those
students "who strongly accepted" and those "who
strongly opposed" traditional religious doctrines, and
gave them the ACE Psychological Examination, 1945
edition, an intelligence test. They reported that,
"The mean ACE score of 119 for Non-Believers was
considerably and significantly higher than the mean
scores of 98 and 100 for Believers and Bible students
respectively....The mean percentile rank of Non-
Believers was 80, while that of believers and Bible
students clustered around 50. The differences of 27
and 30 percentile points approximated the difference
reported by Howells," which Brown and Lowe reported
was 25 percentile points (Brown and Lowe, 1951: 122-
23). They claimed that their findings "strongly cor-
roborate those of Howells."
They also reported that the inverse correlation
between intelligence and religiosity was much higher
among upperclassmen than among lowerclassmen. The
mean intelligence test score of junior and senior non-
believers was 29.75 percentile points above that of
junior and senior believers, while the difference for
freshmen and sophomores was only 17.50. The widening
of this difference was probably due in part to
increase in average native intelligence, as well as to
two more years of education.

11. Argyle, 1958

In his book, Religious Behavior (1958), Michael
Argyle briefly reviewed the literature on the correlation between student intelligence and religious faith

and concluded that, "Although intelligent children grasp religious concepts earlier, they are also the first to doubt the truth of religion, and intelligent students are much less likely to accept orthodox beliefs..." He explained this by asserting that, "Intelligent people are less amenable to social pressure..." which implies that there is social pressure to profess orthodox religious beliefs (p. 96). He failed to suggest a more important reason, namely that religious beliefs may seem to be irrational.

Argyle noted that, while the above studies apply only to students, similar conclusions "may hold for adults as well, since authoritarianism (which correlates with religious conservatism) is correlated with IQ to the extent of -.2 to -.5 (Christie and Jahoda, 1954: 168)" (Argyle, 1958: 93).

12. Bryant, 1958

In 1958, M. D. Bryant completed an unpublished doctoral dissertation at the University of Nebraska entitled "Patterns of Religious Thinking of University Students as Related to Intelligence." I have not read it. According to Clyde A. Parker, Bryant interviewed or questionaired 104 students — 52 superior and 52 average — asking 25 questions on 5 areas of religious thought, and found that: "(a) First-year university students of high intellectual ability are more similar, with regard to religious thinking, to fourth-year students of high and average ability than they are to first-year students of average ability, and (b) educational advancement from first to fourth year... indicates change from conservative religious thinking to more liberal thoughts" (Parker, 1971: 742-43). Together these conclusions clearly imply that "intellectual ability" varies inversely with amount of religious faith.

According to Feldman and Newcomb (1969; 31) the 52 intellectually superior students scored 9.96, and the 52 average students scored 9.38, on Bryant's test of religious liberalism. These data indicate that his superior students believed less than his average students.

13. Kosa and Schommer, 1961

In 1961 John Kosa and Cyril O. Schommer, S.J., reviewed some of the studies supporting the conclusion that intelligence varies inversely with religiosity, and suggested that their own research cast doubt on this conclusion. They polled 362 white male students in a Catholic college on their knowledge of religious doctrine, and found, as one would expect, that the most intelligent students made the highest scores (Kosa and Schommer, 1961: 91). They implied, but did not explicitly assert, that their research undermined the conclusions of previous researchers. However, this implication is unjustified, both because knowledge of doctrine is quite different from belief in it, and because the sample of students surveyed was not a representative sample.

14. Hadden, 1963

In 1963 sociologist Jeffrey K. Hadden (University of Wisconsin) reported on a survey of 261 UW seniors who were given an unnamed and undescribed religiosity test. He reported that "there is no correlation between grade point average and the conventional religiosity index" (Hadden, 1963: 214). In fact he found an insignificant −.03 correlation (p. 212).

Since grade point averages are closely correlated with intelligence scores, this is an anomalous finding. I suspect that he found no significant correlation because GPA scores are an imperfect measure of intelligence and/or because his religiosity index was a poor index of religious belief.

Hadden explained his unusual finding by the fact that his seniors were homogeneous in intelligence, having "been selected on the basis of intellectual performance." This is a very unsatisfactory explanation.

15. Young, Dustin, and Holtzman, 1966

In 1958 and 1964 Wayne H. Holtzman, Robert K. Young and their associates at the University of Texas used a 23-item questionnaire to measure "attitudes toward organized religion" among 1074 students. Their questionnaire consisted of 23 statements, and allowed 5 alternative reactions to each statement (ranging from "strongly agree" to "strongly disagree"). Possible scores ranged from 0, the most negative, to 92, the most positive attitude. They also determined grade-point averages and determined mean scores for each of five groups—below C, C+, B-, B+, and A-. This allowed the determination of correlations.

They reported that in 1958 the religious scores varied directly with the grade-point scores, but only very slightly—from 60.6 to 63—and all of this variation occurred in the first step, from "Below C"

(30 students) to "C+" (158 students). In 1964, however, there was a much larger and more continuous
inverse correlation between the religious and grade-
point scores. The religious scores fell continuously
from 57.0 for "below C" students to 51.6 for 102 B+
students, and then rose to 53.9 for 39 A- students.
The average religious score for the B+ and A- students
was 52.2, compared with 56.8 for the C and C+ groups
combined (Young et al, 1966: 44).

The slight and abnormal positive correlation
reported for 1958 may have been due to the still lin-
gering effects of McCarthyism on college teaching and
student response.

16. Trent, 1967

In 1963 James W. Trent polled 1400 college seniors
in over 100 schools in 16 communities in the Midwest,
California, and Pennsylvania, where they had been
studied as high school seniors. The college seniors
were tested for both religious liberalism and academic
aptitude. He reported that 712 non-Catholic seniors
rated "high" in ability had a mean score of 50.2 on
religious liberalism while 65 non-Catholic seniors
rated low in ability had a mean score of 47.3, which
indicated that the most able were the least religious
(Trent, 1967: 194).

Unfortunately his high-ability group included
64% of all his subjects. If he had selected the 10%
or 20% who were the most able, the difference in the
religious scores would probably have been much greater.

17. Plant and Minimum (1967)

In 1960 C. W. Telford and W. T. Plant gave California Psychological Inventory intelligence tests and
Allport-Vernon-Lindsey religious value tests to 926
male applicants for admission to six public junior
colleges in California. In 1962 all were retested.
The AVL religious-value test is a weak test of religious belief.

In 1967 Plant and E. W. Minium analyzed the data
collected by Telford and Plant. They calculated
separate mean religious value scores for the 228
students who ranked in the upper 25%, and for the 216
students who ranked in the lower 25%, on the basis of
their intelligence tests. They reported that the more
intelligent students were less religious, both before
entering college (religious value scores 38.3, compared to 39.0) and after two years of college (36.8

and 38.9). The most intelligent students were most
influenced by their college experience (Plant and
Minium, 1967: 145).

18. Wuthnow, 1978

In 1970-72 the Institute for Research in Social
Behavior (UC, Berkeley) polled about 2000 freshmen and
senior students at UC Berkeley on their religious
views, and also obtained the entering student aptitude
test (SAT) scores on each student. In 1978 Robert
Wuthnow published a report on the relationship of the
religious views to the SAT scores of 532 of these
students (all males). He found that, of the students
he classified as Christians, only 37% scored above
average on the verbal SAT, while 58% of the apostates,
and 44% of the nonreligious, did so. On the math SAT,
the figures were 45%, 58%, and 53% respectively
(Wuthnow, 1978: 159). These data support the conclusion that intelligence varies inversely with amount of
religious faith.

19. Hastings and Hoge, 1967, 1974

In both 1967 and 1974, Philip K. Hastings and
Dean Hoge polled about 200 Williams College students
on their religious beliefs and related attitudes, and
correlated the results with data on the students'
scholastic aptitude scores. They found no significant
correlation, and reported that this finding was new.
"Virtually all studies done prior to World War II
found significant correlations between higher test
scores and religious liberalism, often as high as .2
or .3" (Hastings and Hoge, 1976:248). Moreover, I
hereby review ten postwar studies, all but two of
which reported a negative correlation between some
measure of intelligence and amount of religious faith.
Therefore, I believe that Hastings and Hoge's finding
was very atypical, perhaps because they gave undue
weight to attitudes.

20. Poythress, 1975

In 1972 Richard A. Hunt argued that earlier conclusions concerning the correlation between intelligence and religiosity were "at best meaningless and,
at most, dangerous and misleading" because they failed
to give due weight to the views of proreligious, non-
fundamentalist believers.

To test this hypothesis, Normal G. Poythress of
the University of Texas polled some 200 of his intro-

ductory psychology students on their religious beliefs, classified them according to the degree and kind of their religious faith, and then determined the correlations between SAT scores, a rough measure of intelligence, and religious faith for each of his eight classes of respondents. He concluded that his results did not support Hunt's charges but instead confirmed the conclusion of nearly all previous researchers. He reported that the 33 pollees he classified as "strongly antireligious" (Group E) had a 12% higher mean SAT score (1148) than that (1022) for all 139 religious pollees (Groups A,B,C,D). The SAT scores for the 15 "moderately antireligious" (1119) and the 24 "slightly antireligious" respondents (1108) were also higher than that for the religious ones (Poythress, 1975: 277-75).

21. Wiebe and Fleck, 1980

In 1980 Ken F. Wiebe and J. R. Fleck, of the Rosemead Graduate School of Professional Psychology, published a study of the personality correlates of 158 male and female Canadian university students. They used questionnaires to classify them as intrinsically religious (fundamentalists), extrinsically religious (liberals), and nonreligious, and gave them intelligence tests. They reported that "nonreligious S's tended to be strongly intelligent," and "more intelligent than religious S's." They also found that religious liberals resembled the nonreligious subjects much more closely than they resembled the religious conservatives (Wiebe and Fleck, 1980: 182). In other words, they found that religious faith varied inversely with intelligence.

22. Comments

I have now reviewed 21 different studies of the relationship between individual student intelligence and religious belief, all but four of which (Corey, Gilliland, Hadden, Hastings and Hoge) support the conclusion that intelligence varies inversely, but far less than proportionally, with some measure of religiosity. No one has reported a significant positive correlation between IQ and faith. Unfortunately, no researcher has ever tried to replicate Howell's brilliant pioneer study. Instead, each subsequent researcher has used a new and less perfect methodology.
These 21 studies are more directly relevant to the relationship of intelligence to religious belief than any other studies, both because they dealt with

the correlation between individual intelligence and individual belief, and because they were the least affected by differences in the amount of education. In each study, all students had about the same number of years of education.

Since there are so few such directly relevant studies, especially in recent years, it is worthwhile to review some less relevant studies.

B.   Student Body Comparisons

Several studies have found that students in the most prestigious colleges are much less religious than those in the less prestigious schools. Since the average native intelligence of students in the best schools is higher than that of students in other schools, it is reasonable to attribute much of the difference in amount of religious faith to differences in native intelligence. They cannot be largely due to differences in length of education because the groups compared have had about the same number of years of formal education. Of course, they can be partly due to differences in the quality of precollege and college education.

1.   Goldsen's Cornell Values Study, 1960

In 1952 a Cornell University research group, led by Rose K. Goldsen, conducted a survey of values among some 4800 male students in eleven American colleges and universities. This Cornell values study included questions on religion. The answers revealed that the amounts of both religious belief and religious behavior varied inversely with the quality of the school. For instance, the percent of students who claimed to "believe in a Divine God" rose from 30% at Harvard to 45% at the University of Michigan and to 68% at the University of North Carolina, as shown in Table 1 (Goldsen et al, 1960: 158).

TABLE 1

Student Belief in a Divine God, 1952

	%		%
Harvard	30	Wesleyan	43
UCLA	32	Michigan	45
Dartmouth	35	Fisk	60
Yale	36	Texas	62
Cornell	42	N. Carolina	68
Wayne	43		

2. Stark, 1963

In 1958 the National Opinion Research Center (NORC) of the University of Chicago polled 2842 graduate students in 25 U.S. Ph.D.-granting universities, and included questions on religious affiliation and involvement. Students were asked to rate their religious involvement as high, low, or none.

In 1963 Rodney Stark (UC, Berkeley) published an analysis of the data collected in this poll. He classified both the schools where these students had graduated, and the schools they were attending as high, medium, or low in academic quality, which enabled him to correlate the degree of each students religious involvement with the quality of the student's undergraduate school, and also with that of the school where the student was a graduate student. He found that in both cases the quality of the school varied inversely with the degree of student religious involvement. In his words, the degree of "religious involvement declines as the quality of the graduate school rises," and "religious involvement increases as the quality of undergraduate training decreases." For instance, among students who had graduated from high-quality universities, only 20% related their religious involvement as "high," and 41% as "none;" while, among those who had graduated from low-quality universities, 48% rated their religious involvement as "high," and only 25% as "none" (Stark, 1963: 17-18). These conclusions were elaborated in a 1965 book by Charles Y. Glock and R. Stark.

3. Zelan, 1968

The 1958 NORC poll asked questions about the religious identification of pollees and their parents. In 1968 Joseph Zelan, sociologist from the University of California at Davis, published an analysis of the high apostasy rates revealed by this poll. He reported that, "The proportion of apostates, those who had left their parents' church, among those who attended elite colleges is 33%; among those who attended other colleges, 21%" (Zelan, 1968: 372). Most apostates joined more liberal churches or none.

4. National Review Study, 1970

The conclusion that student religious belief varies inversely with the quality of the students and the school was again confirmed by a 12-school survey

of student belief among sophomores, juniors, and
seniors conducted by the conservative National Review,
in 1969-70. Some of the findings of this poll (NR,
6-13-71: 650) are shown in Table 2.

TABLE 2

Students Belief in a Spirit or Personal God, 1969

	%		%
Reed	15	Yale	42
Brandeis	25	Howard	47
Sarah Lawrence	28	Indiana	57
Williams	36	Davidson	59
Stanford	41	S. Carolina	65
Boston Univ.	41	Marquette	77

Some of these differences in religious faith are
due to causes other than differences in IQ and education—for instance, to the proportions of Jews and
Catholics in the student body—but differences in
native intelligence are probably a major cause.

5. Caplovitz and Sherrow, 1977

In the years 1961-63 the National Opinion Research
Center polled some 34,000 college seniors in many
different U.S. colleges, and included questions on
both current religious identification and that of their
parents. In 1977 David Caplovitz and Fred Sherrow
published an analysis of the apostasy rates revealed
by this NORC survey. They reported that these rates
varied directly with the quality of the college.
They used the measure of school quality employed
by Lazarsfeld in The Academic Mind, and reported that
apostasy rates rose continuously from 5% for "low"
ranked schools to 8% for "medium low," to 10% for
"medium high," and to 17% for "high" ranked schools—
Harvard, Yale, Columbia, Berkeley, etc. (Caplovitz,
1977: 111).

6. Greeley, 1970

A. M. Greeley analyzed some of the NORC 1961 poll
data. He segregated the 2159 Protestant college
seniors who planned to begin graduate work in arts
and sciences the following year, and reported that
the apostasy rate for this select, high-IQ group was

31%, over twice as high as the 15% rate for 2007
Protestant seniors (a 10% sample) who did not plan to
begin graduate work (Greeley, 1070: 341). The 15%
rate, of course, was probably far above that for 22-
year olds who had not gone to college, and had a much
lower average IQ.

7. Niemi, Ross, and Alexander, 1978

In 1978 R. G. Niemi, R. D. Ross, and J. Alexander
published a study of a representative sample of
college students in each of a variety of schools,
including "nine elite institutions." They reported
that, in these elite schools, "organized religion was
judged important" by only 26% of the students, compared
with 44% for all students polled. Moreover, only 24%
of those in elite schools "felt that abortion is
morally wrong," while the figure for all students polled was 43% (Niemi et al, 1978: 513).

8. ACE, 1982

The American Council on Education (ACE) has polled
over 140,000 entering freshment in many U.S. colleges
and universities each year since 1967. One of the
questions asked for current religious preference, and
the answers are classified as Protestant, Catholic,
Jewish, other, or none. The schools have been classified according to their selectivity, using average
combined SATV and SATM scores. The four-year private,
nonsectarian colleges were classified as low selectivity (less than 950), medium selectivity, high
selectivity, and very high selectivity (1175+). In
1982, in the low selectivity colleges, only 8.7% of
the freshmen reported no religious preference. In the
very high selectivity colleges, 19.1% did so (ACE,
1982: 83). These data strongly imply that, on average,
the most intelligent students are the least religious.

9. Comments

I have now reviewed seven different studies comparing
different college and university student bodies on the
basis of average religiosity and average intellectual
quality and one other group study (Greeley). All
studies found that religiosity tends to vary inversely
with the intellectual quality of the student body, or
group. This unanimous finding strongly supports the
conclusion that, among college students, intelligence
varies inversely with religiosity.

C.   The Religious Faith of College Professors

As a class, college professors score much higher on intelligence tests than the average man (over 130 compared with 100).   Therefore, if their religious views differ markedly from those of the average man, these differences are probably due in large part to differences in native intelligence, as well as to differences in education.   There is considerable and unanimous evidence that college professors are much less religious than other college alumni and adults in general.   Since I have reviewed such evidence in Chapter II (Section B), I need not review it again here.

D.   Studies of Very-High-IQ Groups

I turn now to studies of the religiosity of persons belonging to other groups with very high minimum and average IQs.   The mean IQ for the subjects covered here is probably well over 150.

1.   Terman, 1959

In 1922 Lewis M. Terman of Stanford, the intelligence test pioneer, began a still-continuing study of a group of very gifted (IQ 140+) students then in high school.   In a 1959 book, The Gifted Group at Mid-Life (pp. 116-7) he classified his subjects into four groups according to their religious inclination— "strong, moderate, little, and none at all."   He reported that only 10% of the men and 18% of the women had a "strong" religious inclination, while 62% of the men and 57% of the women claimed "little" religious inclination or "none at all" (28% and 23%).
As noted earlier, a 1976 Gallup national poll allowed four similar choices, and found that 66% of male adults claimed that religion is "very important" to them; and only 5% that it is "not at all important."

2.   Warren and Heist, 1960

In 1956 Jonathan R. Warren and Paul A. Heist (both of UC, Berkeley) gave personality tests, including the Allport-Vernon-Lindsay (AVL) religious value scale, to about 450 National Merit Scholars (average IQ, 150) and about 450 near-winners (average IQ, 130). They reported that these gifted high school seniors "of both sexes score as high on the religious scale (male, 41.7; female, 46.5) as do any of the groups used here for comparison," namely UC Berkeley freshmen, Michigan State University freshmen, and "other" college students (Warren and Heist, 1960: 335).

They apparently recognized that their finding was inconsistent with most previous relevant findings, but they did not report these findings, or try to explain the conflict with them. This conflict may be partly due to the fact that they compared high school seniors with college students, to the fact that IQ is only one of several criteria for selecting National Merit Scholarship winners and near winners, to defects of the AVL religious value scale, and/or to other defects in their research methods.

It is possible that those who selected National Merit Scholars gave significant weight, consciously or unconsciously, to degree of religious faith. According to Warren and Heist, the selectors considered "motivation, breadth of interests, accomplishments, personality, and leadership potential," in addition to scholastic aptitude test scores.

It is unfortunate that Warren and Heist did not report separate average religious scores for the NMS winners (average IQ 150), the near winners (average IQ 130), and the average 18-year old (IQ 100).

3. Southern and Plant, 1968

In 1968 Mara L. Southern and Walter T. Plant published a study of 42 male and 30 female U.S. members of Mensa—mean age 36, mean IQ 170+, mean education 15.7 years—who had taken the Allport-Vernon-Lindsay test of personal values (AVL). They reported that on the AVL religious scale the Mensa males' mean score was 27.9, and the female mean 31.3, far below the Warren-Heist AVL norm of 40.0 for college students, which implies that these American Mensa members were much less religious in belief than the typical American college alumnus or adult (Southern and Plant, 1968: 122).

It is noteworthy that these Mensa AVL religious scores were also far below those reported by Warren and Heist for NMS winners and near winners, probably chiefly because their mean IQ was much higher.

4. Comments

The authors of two of the three studies reviewed in this section concluded that persons with a very high IQ were much less religious than persons with a normal IQ, and the dissenting study did not report a positive

correlation between IQ and faith. In these studies
the high IQ subjects had more formal education, which
certainly explains part of the difference in religiosity. Nevertheless, these two studies are consistent
with the conclusion that the amount of religious faith
varies inversely with native intelligence.

E. Studies of Success and Religiosity

As previously explained, since so few researchers
have studied the correlation between individual IQ
scores and religiosity, it is worth examining studies
which reveal the relationship between average group
religiosity scores and factors positively correlated
with IQ scores. Success or achievement in life is one
such factor, and the correlation between such success
and religiosity has been studied by several researchers. A review of their studies follows. It includes
all such studies known to me, except those by Professor
James H. Leuba, which I reported in detail in Chapter
II. Leuba found that eminent U.S. scientists were much
less religious than other scientists, who in turn were
far less religious than other U.S. adults.

1. W. S. Ament, 1927

In a 1926 Scribner's Magazine article, C. C. Little
(President, University of Michigan) reported on the
results of a check of certain names in Who's Who in
the U.S. He found that, "Unitarians, Episcopalians,
Congregationalists, Universalists, and Presbyterians
are...far more numerous in Who's Who than would be
expected on the basis of the population which they
form. Baptists, Methodists, and Catholics are distinctly less numerous..." (Ament, 1927: 399).
Since persons whose names appear in Who's Who
have an average IQ score far above that of other
persons, and since "Unitarians, Episcopalians, Congregationalists, Universalists, and Presbyterians are
more liberal in their religious beliefs than "Baptists,
Methodists and Catholics," Little's data suggest that
religious liberals are more intelligent than religious
conservatives.
In order to check Little's finding, Wm. S. Ament
of Scripps College reviewed the latest Marquis Who's
Who in the U.S. data on 2000 listed persons (10% of
the total), and determined the relative frequency of
such persons for each of 12 denominations. His findings confirmed Little's conclusion. He reported that,
in proportion to number, the liberal sects have
supplied many more individuals in Who's Who than the

conservative sects. For instance, he found that Unitarians, by far the least religious, were over 40 times as numerous in Who's Who as in the U.S. population (Ament, 1927: 461).

2. Lehman and Witty, 1931

To further check Little's finding, Harvey C. Lehman (Ohio University) and Paul A. Witty (Northwestern) identified 1189 scientists listed both in Who's Who (1926-27) and as eminent in American Men of Science (1927). Only 25% of these eminent scientists, and 50% of all those listed in this Who's Who, reported their religious denomination in Who's Who, although the Who's Who editors had specifically asked them to report "religious denomination (if any)." Since 97% of U.S. adults claimed a religious affiliation in 1953, the 25% figure for these eminent scientists suggests that they were far less religious than the average American adult.

Moreover, Lehman and Witty reported that those "who give information regarding church affiliation are associated in most instances with the relatively liberal denominations." For instance, they found that Unitarians were 81.4 times as numerous among these eminent scientists as the average non-Unitarian (Lehman and Witty, 1931: 545-48).

3. Kelley and Fiske, 1951

In his book, Religious Behavior (1958), Argyle reported (p. 95) on a study by E. L. Kelley and D. W. Fiske. They studied the relationship between the strength of the religious value and research competence among clinical psychologists, and found a negative correlation of -.39. I have been unable to obtain a copy of their book, The Selection of Clinical Psychologists (1951).

4. Ann Roe, 1953

In 1953 Anne Roe, a clinical psychologist, published the results of her personal psychological analysis of 64 eminent U.S. scientists, nearly all members of the prestigious National Academy of Science or of the American Philosophical Society. She reported that while nearly all of them had religious parents and had attended Sunday School, "now only three of these men are seriously active in church. A few others attend upon occasion, or even give some financial support to a church which they do not attend.... All the others have long since dismissed religion as any guide to them, and the church plays no part in their lives.... A few are militantly atheistic, but most are just not interested" (Roe, 1953: 61).

5. Francis Bello, 1954

In order to determine "What kind of a man becomes an outstanding scientist?" Francis Bello interviewed or questionnaired 107 young (40 or under) nonindustrial American scientists judged by their senior colleagues to be outstanding. He received 87 replies, and published his findings in Fortune (June, 1954). He asked questions about religious beliefs and affiliation, and found that his respondents were far less religious in belief and affiliation than their parents and the U.S. public. For instance 45% of the 87 subjects claimed to be "agnostic or atheistic," and an additional 22% claimed no religious affiliation. Moreover, Bello reported that, for the 20 most eminent subjects, "the proportion who are now a-religious is considerably higher than in the [entire] survey group" (p. 143).

6. Chambers, 1964

In 1963 Jack A. Chambers, University of South Florida, sent questionnaires to 740 male U.S. psychologists and chemists (half already recognized as eminent) in order to determine the personality traits of creative scientists. On the basis of his data he reported that "The highly creative men...significantly more often show either no preference for a particular religion or little or no interest in any religion;..." (Chambers, 1964: 1203-05). He found that the creative (i.e. eminent) scientists were very much less religious than the non-eminent. For instance, 43% of the eminent psychologists had "no religious preference," though only 6% of their parents, and 17% of the non-eminent psychologists, were so classified (Chambers, 1965: 67). Moreover, although the chief arguments for religious faith are psychological, the eminent psychologists were far less religious than the eminent chemists—40% no preference versus 16%. All of these findings confirm Leuba's pioneer discoveries, but Chambers did not mention his work.

7. Vaughan, Smith, and Sjoberg, 1965

In 1959-60 T. R. Vaughan, D. H. Smith, and G. Sjoberg polled some 850 U.S. physicists, zoologists, chemical engineers, and geologists listed in American Men of Science (1955) on their church memberships, attendance patterns, and belief in an afterlife. They received 642 usable replies.

The replies revealed that 38.5% of these scientists did not believe in life after death, and that only 31.8% believed in it. Moreover, belief in immortality was lower among scientists employed by "major universities," presumably the most eminent, than among those employed by business, government, and "minor universities." The authors explained that the former "may be less constrained by community or other social bonds" (Vaughan et al, 1965: 521, 525). I would suggest that these least religious scientists probably had both more and/or better education and higher IQs.

According to several Gallup polls, about two thirds of U.S. adults believe in life after death, so the scientists covered by this study were far less religious than the typical U.S. adult.

8. Bender, 1968

In 1965 Irving E. Bender, a Dartmouth College psychologist, retested 96 of 112 Dartmouth graduates (class of 1940) and classified them as 59 church attenders and 37 nonattenders. Most of them had been successful in life. He found no significant difference between attenders and non-attenders with respect to college grades, but that "a statistically reliable difference favors nonattenders" on (1) their freshman Scholastic Aptitude test, (2) on their senior Graduate Record Examination, and (3) on Bender's estimate of creativity (Bender, 1968: 234-35). It is well established that adults who attend church are more religious in faith than nonattenders.

9. Gallup, Jr., 1982

According to George Gallup, Jr., a 1982 Gallup poll on belief in life after death revealed that, while 67% of Americans believe in such life, only 32% of "leaders in medicine" and only 16% of "leading scientists" so believe (G. Gallup, Jr., 1982, 47-48). I have been unable to find a detailed published version of this poll.

Of course, much of these wide differences in belief is due to differences in amount of formal education, but much also is probably due to differences in native intelligence.

F.   Other Gallup Polls

U.S. public opinion polls conducted by the American Institute of Public Opinion, the Gallup polls, have almost uniformly shown that college alumni (average IQ 115) are much less likely to support religious dogmas on God, immortality, hell, prayer, creation, abortion, etc., than are other U.S. adults (average IQ 97). In Chapter II, Section C, "The Effect of Education on U.S. Adult Religious Faith," I reported the findings of many such adult polls, and therefore will not report them individually again here.

G.   Studies of College Classes

In Chapter II, Section A, I also reviewed many studies which revealed that college seniors are less religious than juniors, juniors than sophomores, and sophomores than freshmen. Since these studies are numerous, and are primarily relevant to the effect of education on religious faith, I will not review them again here. I wish only to note that the reported decline in religious faith with each year of additional education is probably due in part, a small part, to the fact that some of the least intelligent students drop out each year as the process of formal education continues. Moreover, the IQs of many college students rise with age. Therefore, these studies of the effect of education on religiosity provide some weak evidence that religious faith varies inversely with intelligence, as well as with amount of formal education.

H.   Aging and Religious Faith

Many studies have shown that, at any given time, IQ scores vary inversely with age after about age 24, and that the decline in IQ is much more rapid after age 65 (Berelson and Steiner, 1964: 221). Other studies, including several Gallup polls, have consistently revealed that, at any given time, old people, especially the very old, are much more religious than young people (Argyle, 1958: 67-69). For instance, a Gallup poll on the origins of the Bible revealed that only 24% of pollees age 25-29 believed that "the Bible is the actual word of God and is to be taken literally, word for word." The percentage of belief rose steadily with age to 42% for those age 50-64, and to 47% for those 65 or older (Gallup Poll, 1982b: 174). If a separate figure for those over 80 had been calculated, it would probably have been 5 to 10 percentage points higher, as Argyle's 1958 review suggests.

The fact that adults over age 24 become both less intelligent and more religious in faith each year as they grow older is perfectly consistent with the findings of the vast majority of studies on the correlation between native intelligence and amount of religious faith. However, intelligence is probably not the chief factor responsible for the positive correlation between age and religious faith. The aged have received much less secondary and higher education than people age 25 to 45, and this may be a more significant factor than their lower intelligence.

I.   Conclusions

In this chapter I have reviewed: (1) 21 studies of the correlation between individual measures of student intelligence and religiosity, all but 4 of which reported an inverse correlation, (2) 8 studies reporting that student bodies or groups with high average IQ and/or SAT scores are much less religious than inferior student groups, (3) 6 studies reporting that college professors (average IQ 125+) are much less religious than the general adult public (average IQ 100), (4) 2 studies reporting that geniuses (average IQ 150+) are much less religious than the general public, and one dubious dissenting study, (5) 9 studies reporting that highly successful persons are much less religious in belief than are other men. All but 5 of these 47 studies support the conclusion that native intelligence varies inversely with degree of religious faith, i.e., that, other factors being equal, the more intelligent a person is, the less religious in faith he is.

I have also noted that many studies reviewed in Chapter II have shown that students become less religious in faith as they proceed through college, probably in part because their average IQ rises, and/or that, among adults, the best educated are much less religious than the least educated, probably in part because the best educated have a much higher mean IQ.

I am sure I have missed some relevant studies, but I believe I have found over 90% of them, and I have not ignored any study because its conclusions were unusual.

106

J. Explanation

So far I have restricted my discussion to factual conclusions based upon scientific research on the correlation between intelligence and religious faith in the U.S. It is time to suggest briefly the chief reasons for the negative correlation between them.

In every society nearly all children and youth are taught to accept traditional religious, moral, political, and other social beliefs. Only a minority, the most intelligent and/or best educated, become dissenters, and dissenters often find it expedient to conceal their dissent. In advanced countries, religious dissenters are now more free than ever before to express their dissent, and that is one of the reasons why more and more of the most intelligent and best educated people have openly rejected some or all traditional religious dogmas.

In my opinion, however, the chief reason for this growing rejection of basic religious dogmas by the most intelligent people is that all purely religious dogmas are senseless, and therefore irrational. It is impossible to conceive of any way to use sensory data to determine whether any such dogmas is factually true or false. In other words, it makes no observable and practical difference whether any religious dogmas is true or false. It is therefore irrational or illogical to claim that any purely religious dogma is true or false. A senseless proposition cannot be true or false.

Other factors being equal, the more intelligent a person is, and/or the longer his formal education, the less likely he is to believe in any irrational theory. If purely religious dogmas are senseless and irrational, this goes far to explain why the most intelligent and most educated men are the least likely to accept them.

Although all purely religious dogmas are senseless and irrational, some theories widely accepted as religious dogmas are verifiably false. For instance, creationism, the doctrine that the universe and all living beings were created in a few days a few thousand years ago, has been proven to be false. Such religious doctrines are first rejected by the most intelligent and/or most educated persons because such persons are the first to learn about and understand the disproof of these theories. But religion would not be fundamentally weakened by general rejection of all such disproven theories. The essential and vital part of modern religious faith is belief in senseless and irrational

107

dogmas such as the existence of a personal God who observes and rewards or punishes our conduct. These beliefs are irrational, but they are not false.

CHAPTER IV.

THE FUTURE OF U.S. RELIGIOUS FAITH

All scientific knowledge makes possible more or less reliable prediction of future events. A scientific hypothesis cannot be verified or disproven unless it implies a verifiable prediction. Therefore, if the conclusions based upon the data reviewed in this book are true, they must imply certain predictions about the future of U.S. religious faith. This chapter is devoted to a statement and justification of such predictions.

In 1794 the Marquis de Condorcet (1743-94), the first and the greatest futurist, confidently predicted that the continued growth of knowledge and education would result in a long and continuous decline in religious faith. "The time will therefore come when the sun will shine only on free men who know no other master but their reason, when...priests...will exist only in works of history and on the stage..." (Condorcet, 1979: 179).

Fortunately for his reputation as a futurist, he did not predict how soon this result would occur. In essence, he merely predicted a long-continued decline in religious faith. And this prediction has been fully verified to date. In 1794 the percent of the French who believed in life after death was probably over 95%. By 1975 it had fallen to 39% (G. H. Gallup, 1976: 18). And the religious editor of Newsweek reported in 1977 (Oct. 10, p. 69) that, "according to a recent public opinion poll, fully 30% of all French citizens between 15 and 30 profess no religious belief at all." Barrett estimates that the percent of the world population which is "non-religious and atheist rose from 0.2% in 1900 to 20.8% in 1980" (Time, 5-3-82, p. 66).

A. Reasons Why U.S. Religious Faith Will Decline

The most important general prediction which is supported by the data reviewed in this book is that religious faith in both the U.S. and the world as a whole will continue to decline indefinitely, i.e., as far as we can see into the future. My chief general reason for making this prediction is that religious faith has long been declining, and that the same factors which caused the long past decline will continue to operate indefinitely in the future. I shall now list, and then discuss, the chief of these factors, roughly in the order of their importance. They are:

1. The growth of knowledge

2. The growth of formal education

3. The growth of informal education

4. The growth in the influence of very intelligent persons

5. The growth of freedom of expression

6. Economic progress

7. The improvement of health care

8. Progress in social reform

9. The rise of logical positivism or scientism

I shall now explain each of these causal factors.

1. The growth of knowledge has long tended to weaken religious faith. For instance, acceptance both of the idea that the earth is not the center of the universe and of the theory that human beings have evolved from lower animals caused many people to abandon some or all religious beliefs. Scientific knowledge is certain to continue to grow, and will enable men to explain and/or control ever more events without relying on supernatural beings or forces.

2. The continued growth and improvement of formal education will indefinitely increase the average person's understanding of both the old and the new scientific knowledge that enables people to solve their personal and social problems without believing in and relying upon supernatural spirits and help. In the absence of widespread education, knowledge has relatively little effect on the belief of the masses.
Even without any further growth of education, the past education of parents and future parents will continue to reduce the religious faith of their children, through home influence, for at least one more generation, and probably longer. Several studies reviewed in

Chapter II above revealed that college students whose parents had been to college were less religious than their fellow students. Future research will confirm this conclusion, and also will probably reveal that grandchildren are affected by the formal education of their grandparents.

3. Informal education is largely the result of reading books and periodicals, listening to the radio, and watching TV programs. There has been a vast and continuous growth of such education for many decades, and such education is likely to continue to grow and improve indefinitely. It probably has much the same effect as formal education.

4. As demonstrated in Chapter III, the more intelligent people are, the less religious they are. It is highly unlikely that the average native intelligence of any large population will change significantly in the next 100 years. It may seem, therefore, that the negative correlation between such intelligence and religious faith will not directly affect future trends in religious faith. However, there will probably be important indirect effects. All of our major institutions of education and information — schools, press, TV, etc. — are dominated by persons of superior intelligence, who have great influence on what is taught, published, and broadcast. Moreover, in every field of human behavior and thought there is a tendency for the less intelligent and successful to imitate the more intelligent and successful. Hence, it is likely that the less intelligent will increasingly accept the religious opinions of the more intelligent, i.e., will become less religious in faith. This trend should occur even among the most intelligent.

The continuing development of ever more efficient methods of selecting intelligent intellectual leaders in our universities, press, and other media, and the constant improvement of media technologies, will steadily increase the already strong influence of the most intelligent people over social and intellectual trends in all countries. Moreover, the continued growth of spontaneous selective eugenic breeding (when gifted students marry each other), especially in elite universities, will steadily increase the proportion of very highly intelligent persons in the U.S. population, which will increase the intellectual influence of such people, who are the least religious of all.

5. Freedom of expression for highly intelligent dissenters will continue to increase. Historically speaking, it is only a short time ago that outspoken religious liberals, dissenters, agnostics, and atheists—who were probably on average very superior in both education and intelligence—were arrested, imprisoned, tortured, and hanged or burned at the stake. Such measures were long effective in slowing the decline of religious faith. They are still used in some Catholic and Moslem countries.

There is still much room for further increase in freedom of expression. The National Opinion Research Center has conducted polls which have repeatedly and consistently revealed that most Americans still believe that atheists should not be allowed to teach in U.S. schools, and that a very large minority of Americans believe atheists should not be allowed to speak in public (Davis, 1978: 82).

6. Until recently the great majority of people in every country lived in poverty, serfdom, or slavery, and had little hope for any great improvement in their economic lot. The industrial revolution and the continued advance of technology have vastly improved the economic and political condition of the common man in all advanced countries, precisely those countries in which the decline of religious faith has gone the farthest. If nuclear wars can be avoided or reasonably limited, such economic progress is almost certain to continue. It will enable more and more people to become educated, and will persuade them to rely ever more confidently on their own personal and social efforts to improve their lot. As a result, they will feel less and less need to believe in, and rely upon, supernatural aid and support. Hope for a better life on earth will continue to replace hope for a better life in heaven.

7. Religion arose and flourished in ages when wars, famines, and plagues repeatedly decimated the population, and doctors could do little or nothing to cure the sick or heal the wounded. In such conditions, men find it easy to believe that magic, sacrifice, prayer, worship, and religious faith can heal the sick. The vast recent improvement in scientific health care has greatly reduced illness and death rates, and thereby weakened the temptation to rely on prayer and religious healing. Further medical progress will continue to produce this effect indefinitely.

8. The past century has been an era of continuous political and social reform in all advanced countries, and such reform will continue indefinitely. Every sound social reform, like the adoption of social insurance, makes life healthier, happier, and more economically secure for millions of people. All such progress reduces the imagined need to appeal to supernatural beings for aid and emotional support.

9. In recent decades English-speaking philosophers and students of scientific method have elaborated new theories of knowledge—analytic philosophy, logical or semantic analysis, operationalism, logical positivism, etc.—which have made it much easier to refute or discredit religious theories and dogmas. The continued improvement and spread of these positivist theories will continue indefinitely to weaken religious faith everywhere.

B. Comment on Wuthnow's Criticism

In a 1976 article on the recent pattern of secularization, Robert Wuthnow (Princeton) argued that recent secularization could not be due to "relatively continuous modernizing processes such as" (among others) "gradual upgrading in education and diffusion of science" because the process of secularization has not been continuous. To prove that it has not been continuous, he offered U.S. data on church construction, contributions, religious degrees awarded, religious books published, church membership, and church attendance from 1950 to 1972 (Wuthnow, 1976: 852-53). But some of these trends are strongly influenced by fluctuations in national income. The fact that spending on new churches rises and falls in brief cycles does not imply that belief in God or the devil rises and falls. Moreover, Wuthnow ignored most of the data concerning the long decline in religious faith before 1950.

C. Group Differences in Religious Faith

Having discussed the major social trends or factors which have caused, and will continue to cause, a long decline of U.S. religious faith, I turn now to list, and then discuss, several significant class, group, and national differences in religious faith which suggest a long further decline in U.S. religious faith. These differences are:

1. The best educated Americans are much less religious in faith than the least intelligent.

2. The most intelligent are far less religious in faith than the least intelligent.

3. Young American adults are much less religious in faith than old Americans.

4. Californians are less religious in faith than other Americans.

5. White Americans are less religious in faith than black and brown Americans.

6. Prosperous Americans are less religious in faith than poor Americans.

7. Men are less religious in faith than women.

8. People in advanced countries are less religious in faith than people in undeveloped countries

9. Europeans are much less religious in faith than Americans.

All of these differences in religiosity are due, of course, to the fact that the factors previously listed have had greater effect on some groups of people than others. For instance, people who are poor, black old, or female have had less education than those who are prosperous, white, young, or male. I turn now to discuss the group differences listed above, beginning with number 3 because the first two items were fully treated in Chapters II and III.

3. Many polls cited earlier have revealed that young Americans are much less religious than old Americans, chiefly because they and their parents are better educated than old Americans and their parents. The young are destined to replace the old, and this alone will steadily reduce the average religiosity of Americans for at least two generations.

4. Most progressive social trends have appeared earlier and/or gone further in California than in most other states. It is therefore significant that a 1983 opinion poll in the San Francisco Bay area (population 4.5 million) revealed that only 41% of the nearly 700 respondents classified themselves as Christians, that

19% called themselves nonreligious humanists, and that 12% called themselves atheists or agnostics. The only other large groups, "mystics and spiritualists" (22%), included many persons who believe only in some impersonal force of spirit (S. F. Examiner, April 15, 1983). It will take many decades for the rest of the U.S. to achieve such secularization levels, but this result seems highly probable because it has already been achieved in this California area.

5. Nearly all relevant religious opinion polls have proven that U.S. negroes are much more religious than U.S. whites. For instance, a 1976 Gallup poll revealed that 82% of non-white pollees believed in a God who observes and rewards or punishes people, while the figure for whites was only 66% (G. H. Gallup, 1976: 14). And a 1980 Gallup poll disclosed that 56% of nonwhites believed that the Bible is the "actual word of God," while only 37% of whites so believed (G. H. Gallup, 1981: 187). Continued future emancipation and assimilation of U.S. negroes will make them ever more like whites in culture, including religious faith. This will long tend to reduce the average religiosity of Americans.

6. All relevant Gallup polls have revealed that persons with high incomes are much less religious in faith than persons with low incomes. For instance, a 1981 Gallup Poll found that only 24% of top income receivers ($25,000 plus) believed that the Bible is the "literal word of God," and that 19% of them considered it a "book of fables." For the poorest pollees (under $5,000), the figures were 55% and 9% (G. H. Gallup, 1982b: 174). Since the poor are increasingly adopting the opinions of their richer contemporaries and since average real incomes will continue to rise, this difference in class belief portends a long further decline in U.S. religious faith.

7. Nearly all relevant student and adult polls have found that women are more religious in faith than men. The growing education and emancipation of women will cause them to become more and more like men in their religious beliefs.

8. If we compare the nations of the world by amount and strength of religious belief, it immediately becomes apparent that, the more backward the nation, the more religious it is. For instance, the people of India, sub-Saharan Africa, and Latin America are more

115

religious in faith than are the people of Russia or
the U.S. (G.H. Gallup, 1976: 12). Since most backward
nations will continue to make social progress indefinitely, they will become more and more like advanced
nations in culture and religious faith. Thus the
world as a whole, like the U.S., is almost certain to
become ever less religious in faith.

9. All relevant studies and polls have revealed
that the citizens of advanced European countries are
much less religious than Americans. For instance, in
1968 Gallup International asked people in the U.S. and
in 10 European nations two questions, "Do you believe
in God?" and "Do you believe in life after death?"
For both questions, the "yes" answers were lower in
all countries than in the U.S. For instance, the
percent of "yes" answers in the U.S. were 98 and 73,
while they were only 77 and 38 in the U.K., and 73
and 35 in France (G. H. Gallup, 1972: 2174). A similar
Gallup International poll in 1976 revealed similar
results (G. H. Gallup, 1976: 12). In 1983 the religious editor of Time (10-31-83: 103) reported that "only
6% of West Germans—or for that matter Scandinavians—
worship regularly." The corresponding U.S. figure
is about 40%.

Since European writers and thinkers have long had
great influence on American intellectual trends, it
seems highly likely that this influence will continue,
and that it will help to cause a long further decline
in U.S. religious faith.

D. Reasons Why Americans Are More Religious Than Euro-
     peans

The figures given above clearly prove that
Americans are much more religious in faith than are
Europeans. What are the reasons for this great
difference?

Intellectually, as well as biologically, the U.S.
is a colony or offspring of Europe. Nearly all of
its culture was developed in Europe, and then spread,
often slowly, to America. This is especially true of
very modern or advanced ideas—such as those of the
Enlightenment, the theory of evolution, positivism,
Marxism, and Freudianism. Even the basic theory of
nuclear fission was developed in Europe. It takes
years, often many years, for such new ideas to take
root and flourish in America.

It takes time not only because of the distance
between Europe and America, but also because of the

differences in social conditions, which were far
greater a century or two ago than they are today. New
ideas appear and are first widely accepted in large
cities, not in small towns, and such cities arose in
Europe long before they did so in the U.S. The
American small town or farm of the last century was
not hospitable to intellectuals and critics of religion. The frontier did not breed men like Darwin,
Marx, and Freud, or their followers.

The adoption and long duration of large-scale
Negro slavery in the southern states was also a notable
obstacle to the spread of liberal and sceptical religious ideas. Because of their pitiful situation,
American negroes became, and remain today, the most
religious of all native-born Americans. Moreover, the
slave owners and their white supporters were always
backward in their support of education, especially of
higher education. And competition with negro labor
kept white workers relatively poor, and slowed the
rise of trade unions and liberal political leaders.
As a result, both white and black southerners are
still less educated and more religious than any other
regional group of Americans. The main "Bible belt"
runs across the middle and deep south.

The people of the northern states were, and are,
less religious than those of the south, but they re-
mained more religious than the people of Western
Europe not only because they were long more rural and
isolated from European intellectual trends, but also
because of heavy and continuous immigration of relatively pious peasants, especially from Ireland, Poland,
Italy, and Mexico. Many of these immigrants were
illiterate, and few had even a secondary education.

The growth of industrialism, labor unions, and
the socialist movement in Europe turned millions of
workers against the church, which was often part of
the government and usually supported employers and
conservative politicians against the workers. In
America the churches were independent of the government, were locally controlled by their members, and
were engaged in numerous popular social activities.
In time, many Protestant ministers became quite
liberal in their theology and politics. Thus American
churches became and remain much more popular than
European churches.

Finally, the cold war and the prolonged and
systematic campaign against "atheistic communism" has
probably had much more effect upon both real religious
belief and professions of orthodox religious belief in
the U.S. than in any other advanced country. America

117

has become much more anti-communist than any advanced European country, and atheism is widely associated with communism.

E. The Future Overall Trend in U.S. Religious Faith

The above discussion of the factors and group differences chiefly responsible for the past, and probable future, decline in U.S. religious faith is of course quite incomplete. But I believe it strongly supports the prediction that U.S. religious faith will continue to decline indefinitely.

My expectation that American religious faith will continue its long decline is shared by the Reverend Dr. David Barrett, editor of the World Christian Encyclopedia (1981), the most authoritative survey of world-wide religious trends. He forecast that the number of "nonreligious persons" in the U.S. would rise from 15 to 21 million between 1980 and 2000 A.D. (p. 711).

My confident prediction that American religious faith will continue to decline indefinitely is based on one major assumption, namely that nuclear wars will not devastate America and cause a drastic and permanent fall in U.S. real income per person. Such a catastrophe would radically reduce spending on secondary and higher education, whose growth has been the chief cause of the long past decline in religious faith. It would also make daily life far more painful and dangerous, which would induce many more people to hope for supernatural help and consolation. Therefore, nuclear war may cause a revival of religious faith, if it does not end all human life and faith.

F. Lenski's Bad Prediction

Since 1900, innumerable preachers have optimistically and unscientifically predicted a revival of religion. I ignore their predictions because they were not even allegedly based on scientific evidence. However, a prediction of such a revival by Gerhard Lenski of the University of Michigan deserves consideration because it was apparently based on a review of the relevant literature and data.

In his book, The Religious Factor (1963), Lenski predicted that Catholic church attendance would rise. "The increasing Americanization...the growth of the middle class, the permeation of the working class by middle class values, and the rising level of education are all likely to cause an increase in the proportion

118

of Catholics regularly attending Mass" (p. 47, my italics).

This unfortunate prediction is noteworthy both because it turned out to be a very bad one—from 1966 to 1973 the Mass attendance rate fell by 28% (S.F. Chronicle, 10-28-73, p. 1)—and because it was based in part on the mistaken belief that an increase in education increases religious faith and church attendance. As shown in Chapter II, this belief has repeatedly been disproven.

Moreover, "the increasing Americanization" of U.S. Catholics and "the permeation of the working class by middle-class values" has resulted since 1963 in a rapid growth of artificial birth control, abortion, and divorce among Catholic workers' families, all evidence of a decline in religious faith and behavior.

Lenski asserted that a recent Gallup Poll had shown that church attendance rates were higher for college alumni than for persons with only a grade school education. However, three later Gallup Polls (1974, 1976, 1981) revealed lower attendance rates for college alumni (G. H. Gallup, 1978: 931: 1982a: 44).

G.   The Rate of Future Decline in U.S. Faith

It is difficult to predict the future rate of decline in U.S. religious faith because the rate of decline will be different for each religious dogma and for each group or class of Americans. Moreover, no religious opinion poll on any dogma for any group has been repeated for more than 70 years, and the longest spans cover only college students.

The longest continued studies of the decline in faith among college students report very rapid rates of decline. For instance, James Leuba reported that in College A (Bryn Mawr) the percent of belief in personal immortality fell from 72% in 1914 to 39% in 1933; and that among scientists, it fell from 51% to 33%. According to Hoge, the College A student figure fell from 45% (adjusted) in 1933 to 38% in 1968. The total decline from 1914 to 1968 was 34 points.

Dean Hoge, the chief expert on the decline of U.S. student religious faith, reported in 1974 that "In summary, all studies agree that orthodoxy declined from the late 1940s to 1966-68...The decline was about 13 to 23 points" in all but one college, in about 20 years. These rates of decline were much too rapid to continue indefinitely.

The data on U.S. adult trends suggest much slower rates of decline, but they are far less significant and complete. For instance, there are no nationwide data on the trend in adult belief in a personal God who hears and answers prayers. But the Gallup data on the trend in U.S. belief in life after death suggest a very slow rate of decline. I predict that new and improved adult religious opinion polls will soon reveal a more rapid rate of decline, but one not nearly so rapid as that among U.S. students since 1912.

The most useful data for predicting the rate and amount of decline in U.S. religious faith in a personal God during the next 50 to 100 years are probably those revealing the wide differences in amount of such faith between American college alumni and Americans with 0-8 years education (23 percentage points), and between American and West European adults (24 points in 1976). In 1976 only 44% of West Europeans and 56% of U.S. college alumni claimed to believe in a personal God one who "observes your actions and rewards or punishes you for them." The corresponding U.S. adult figure was 68% (G. H. Gallup, 1976: 12 x 14). It seems very unlikely that Europe is more than a century ahead of America in secularization. Therefore, I predict that the U.S. 68% will decline by 23 percentage points (36%) before the year 2076. This prediction is supported by the fact that in 1983 such religious faith in the San Francisco Bay area had already fallen below my predicted 2076 figure for the entire U.S.

The chief cause of the rapid decline in U.S. religious faith from 1910 to 1980 was the preceding and contemporary growth in the amount of formal education received by the average American. Real spending per person on education in the U.S. rose by some 1000% from 1900 to 1980. The median number of years of formal education per U.S. adult rose by 50% between 1940 and 1980, and probably more than doubled between 1900 and 1980. It seems very unlikely that such abnormally rapid rates of growth can continue. Of course, the effects of this abnormally rapid rate of educational growth will continue for two or more generations, as young people have children and grow old, but the probable future slowdown in education expansion is very likely to eventually cause a marked slowdown in the long-run rate of decline of U.S. religious faith. However, any expansion of formal education, especially higher education, per person, should cause some further decline in religious faith, and other factors, like the growth of knowledge, will have a similar effect.

H.   Predictions on Group Religious Faith Trends

As long as young people continue to have had more formal education than old people, the young will continue to be less religious in faith than the old. But the gap in amount of faith will probably narrow continuously for many decades as the young-old gap in amount of formal education narrows. The rate of growth in U.S. formal education per person was so rapid during the years 1910 to 1980 that it must slow down markedly during the next 100 years, and this slowdown will gradually narrow the young-old education gap for many years. The continued growth of adult education should have the same effect.

In recent years, female enrollment in U.S. colleges and universities has become larger than male enrollment. If female enrollment in secondary and higher schools continues to equal or exceed male enrollment, as seems very likely, the gender gap in religious faith will narrow and eventually disappear before 2050, when old women will be as well educated as old men.

The male gap in religious faith between students in, and alumni of, elite American colleges and universities and students in, and alumni of, third-class schools is unlikely to narrow, indeed it may widen, because it is based largely on differences in IQ, and because elite schools are likely to become even more selective while the lowest ranking schools become still less restrictive in their admission policies.

The gap in religious faith between U.S. high school graduates (age 18) and college graduates (age 22) has long been narrowing, in part because high school teachers have become better educated and more free to criticize conservative religious dogmas like creationism. The growth of informal science education, such as TV science programs, has also probably favored this narrowing. The gap should continue to narrow as the parents and teachers of high school students become better educated and more free to express criticism of religious dogmas. For instance, high school teachers will become increasingly free and able to teach the theories of cosmic, geological, and biological evolution.

The wide gap in religious faith between the most eminent scientists and professors and the least eminent will probably continue to exist, with minor fluctuations, indefinitely because it is based largely on differences in inherited intelligence, not on differences in education or environment. There is little reason to expect that the range of these differences in intelligence will be narrowed in the near future, and it may well widen. Moreover, every refinement of classification will widen the spectrum of difference in faith.

The wide gap in religious faith between Californians and residents of the old South, the Bible Belt, will narrow indefinitely because the inferior schools of the South will probably improve faster than the superior schools of California, because many more Southerners will migrate to California, because national magazines and TV programs will change the South more than the West, and because many more Northern whites will move to the South. There is a universal tendency for cultural differences within each nation to diminish as the means of transportation and communication improve.

The educational gap between U.S. whites and non-whites has long been narrowing, and should continue to narrow indefinitely. This should gradually narrow the wide white-nonwhite gap in amount of religious faith.

The very wide gap in religious faith between the least and most developed nations of the world is very likely to narrow for many decades because the growth of formal education in the least developed countries is likely to be much more rapid than such growth in advanced nations, which have already achieved high levels of education.

The very wide European-American gap in religious faith is also likely to narrow indefinitely because a very large number of factors are gradually reducing cultural differences between these regions. These factors include international travel, trade, communication, etc. Moreover, American scientists and universities have now become as productive and influential as the best European scientists and universities were from 1800 to 1940. Finally, the cold-war McCarthyism which slowed the decline of U.S. religious faith from 1946 to 1960 is likely to continue losing influence in the U.S.

It is useful to classify Americans into three groups on the basis of their religious belief or disbelief, namely (1) fundamentalists, those who accept creationism and most other orthodox religious dogmas, (2) liberals, who reject creationism, hell, devils, etc., and (3) nonbelievers, i.e. atheists and agnostics. The studies reviewed in Chapter I reveal a long past decline in the proportion of Americans who are fundamentalists and a long rise in the proportion who are nonbelievers. I predict that both of these trends will continue indefinitely, both in the U.S. and in the world as a whole.

Past research has proven that the amount of religious faith varies inversely both with IQ and with amount of education, but no research has been done specifically on the combined effect of these two factors. I predict that much future research on this combined effect will be done, and that it will reveal a very wide and growing difference in amount of religious faith between the most intelligent graduates of the most prestigious universities and the least intelligent persons without any secondary education. Moreover, every increase in the detail or fineness of such classification will reveal a wider spectrum of difference. But, even without any change in classification, the difference will probably widen because the most superior group will learn more and faster than the most inferior group.

After their 1956 study of some 900 National Merit Scholars and near-winners (pp. 99-100 above), Warren and Heist concluded that such superior students were as religious in belief as other college students. I predict that future research will prove that such students are markedly less religious in faith than the average college freshman. It will also prove for the first time that National Merit Scholars from elite secondary schools are less religious in faith than those from other secondary schools.

I.   Predictions of Belief in Specific Dogmas

The religious dogma which conflicts most clearly with modern science is the dogma of creationism, the claim that the world and all forms of life were created in their present form in seven days. The percent of belief in this dogma is far lower among young people and educated people than among old people and uneducated people. Therefore, I predict that belief in the dogma of creationism will continue to decline for many decades. By the year 2050 the percent of belief (now 53%) should fall below 30%.

According to a 1975 Gallup poll, the percent of U.S. adult belief in "life after death" was 69 in 1975 (G. H. Gallup, 1976: 18). I predict that this figure will fall below 50 by 2050 A.D.

According to a Catholic Digest Poll, the percent of U.S. adults who believe in "a Hell to which people who have led bad lives and die without being sorry are eternally damned" was 54 in 1965

(p. 71 , above). I predict that this percent will fall
below 40 by 2050 A.D.

    According to a Harris Poll, the percent of U.S.
adults who believe in active euthanasia for terminally
ill patients was 56% in 1981 (p. 29 above). I predict that it will rise above 70% by 2050 A.D. I also
predict that such euthanasia will be legalized in the
U.S., probably before 2050.

    It will be possible to verify or disprove all of
these predictions by means of improved and more fre-
quent future public opinion polls.

    My book, The Next 500 Years, Scientific Predic-
tions of Major Social Trends (1967), contains many
other predictions on future long-run trends in religious faith and behavior (pp. 279-87), all of which I
still believe are sound. However, I shall not repeat
them here because they are not based on the data
reviewed in this book.

J.   Future Research Trends

    Public opinion trends on major social issues
like religion, free education, free health care, etc.,
are very important facts because they explain and help
to predict major historical events. Therefore,
national governments and/or national associations of
historians and social scientists ought to carry out
periodic, uniform, national public opinion polls
designed to reveal trends in public opinion on all
major social issues, including issues which are not
yet widely debated but are likely to become much more
discussed in the future.

    Moreover, historians ought to pay far more
attention to the long-run trends in public opinion on
major issues as soon as these trends have been revealed by a series of reliable public opinion polls.
To date, historians have rarely used opinion poll data
to support their conclusions.

    Although almost everyone agrees that it is
extremely important to know whether religious faith is
rising or falling, no church, nation, or research
institute has yet begun to carry out continuously the
relatively simple and inexpensive research needed to
determine trends in religious faith or behavior. I
am confident that within 50 years some reliable
agency will begin to periodically poll Americans on
their religious faith and behavior. The poll on faith
will include the original Leuba questions and at least
a dozen other religious dogmas, and will allow for at
least five degrees of assent or dissent. It will

be used without any change in the original questions for at least 100 years. It will reveal trends in U.S. religious faith more accurately than ever before. I predict that its use will confirm my forecast of a long further decline in U.S. religious faith. I also predict that historians will greatly increase their use of such opinion polls.

Religious beliefs are but one division of a much larger class of traditional, widely accepted nonscientific beliefs, a class which includes belief in witches, fairies, ghosts, evil spirits, magic, astrology, divination, and other supernatural persons and practices. It seems likely, therefore, that my conclusions and predictions concerning trends in religious faith also apply to trends in belief in most or all other traditional nonscientific beliefs or superstitions.

Many historians have reported a long decline in public acceptance of some or all such nonreligious nonscientific beliefs in advanced countries, and have attributed it to the growth of education and knowledge. Unfortunately, reliable scientific evidence of such a decline is even scarcer than that for the decline of religion. Since 1900, many public opinion polls have included questions on religious faith, but few if any have included questions on belief in witches, fairies, ghosts, etc.

Nevertheless, I confidently predict that such questions will soon be included in scientific nationwide public opinion polls, and will be repeated in the same form over many decades. The data obtained will prove that my major conclusions concerning religious trends and concerning the negative correlation between education and/or intelligence, on the one hand, and faith, on the other, are also valid for faith in most or all traditional nonreligious superstitions. I also predict that these polls will reveal young-old, male-female - white black,and other differences in belief in such traditional superstitions similar to those which I have noted as to group differences in religious faith.

Significant predictions are scientific hypotheses which call implicitly and insistently for specific forms of future research to prove or disprove them. Thus all of my predictions may be used to predict that certain kinds of research will be carried out.

Among significant predictions, the most significant and useful are those which most clearly suggest a specific feasible form of verification, such as a future public opinion poll on belief in certain basic religious dogmas. Thus a prediction that people will become more or less spiritual or more or less materialistic is senseless and useless until a specific method of verification has been suggested, and then its meaning is determined by the proposed method of verification. I have tried to confine my predictions to those which are most obviously and easily verifiable.

POSTSCRIPT

On May 15, 1985, after this book had been set in print, the _San Francisco Chronicle_ published a new Gallup Poll, on premarital sex, which is so typical of U.S. public opinion polls on religious issues that it justifies this postcript.

This poll noted that "There's a lot of discussion about the way words and sexual attitudes are changing..." and asked "what is your opinion about this: Do you think it is wrong for a man and a woman to have sex relations before marriage, or not?" Since nearly all U.S. priests and theologians have always condemned such premarital sex as against God's laws, this is a question of religious faith.

The following table compares the results of this 1985 U.S. poll with a similar Gallup Poll in 1969.

Percent Disapproving Premarital Sex

	1985	1969
National	39%	68%
Men	32	62
Women	44	74
18-29 years	18	49
30-49 years	35	67
50 & older	56	80
Protestants	46	70
Catholics	33	72
College education	31	56
High school	40	69
Grade school	60	77
East	40	65
Midwest	36	69
South	48	78
West	24	55

The data in this table support several of my major conclusions, including: (1) that there has been a marked decline in U.S. religious faith, (2) that each additional year of formal education reduces religious faith, (3) that young adults, who are on average better educated than old adults, are much less religious than old adults, (4) that men, who, on average, are better educated than women, are much less religious than women, (5) that the decline in religious faith has been most rapid among the best educated, (6) that in recent years the decline in religious faith has been much more rapid among U.S. Catholics than among U.S. Protestants, and (7) that the decline in U.S. religious faith has gone much further in the West than in the rest of the country.

On the basis of these data I predict that the percent of U.S. adults who disaprove of premarital sex will fall from the 1985 figure of 39% to or below 24% (the 1985 figure for the west) by the year 2035. I also predict that the like percent for a women will fall from 44% to or below 32%; and for college alumni, from 31% to or below 18%.

REFERENCES

Allport, G. W., J. M. Gillespie, and J. Young
    1948 "The religion of the post-war college
           student." J. of Psychol. 25: 3-33.

Alston, J. P.
    1972 "Socioeconomic correlates of belief."
           J. for the Sci. Study of Religion 2, 2:
           180-82.

Ament, W. S.
    1927 "Religion, education, and distinction."
           School and Society 26: 399-406.

American Council on Education Research Reports

    1968 National Norms for Entering Freshman, Fall,
           1968.
    1969 College and University Faculty, Vol. 5,
           No. 5.
    1972 The American Freshman: National Norms for
           Fall 1972.
    1980 The American Freshman: National Norms for
           Fall, 1980.
    1982 The American Freshman: National Norms for
           1982. Los Angeles: Cooperative Institu-
           tional Research Program.

Argyle, M.
    1958 Religious Behavior. London: Routledge and
           Kegan Paul.

Argyle, M., and B. Beit-Hallahmi
    1975 The Social Psychology of Religion. London:
           Routledge and Kegan Paul.

Arsenian, S.
    1943 "Changes in evaluative attitudes during
           four years of college." J. of Ap. Psychol.
           27: 338-49.

Bain, R.
    1927 "Religious attitudes of college students."
           Am. J. of Sociol. 32: 762-69.

Barrett, D. B.
　　1981 <u>World Christian Encyclopedia</u>. London:
　　　　Oxford University Press.

Baumer, F. L.
　　1960 <u>Religion and the Rise of Scepticism</u>. N.Y.,
　　　　Harcourt, Brace.
　　1977 <u>Modern European Thought.</u> N.Y., Macmillan
　　　　Pub. Co.

Beckwith, B. P.
　　1981 "The Decline in American Religious Faith
　　　　since 1913." <u>Humanist</u> March, 1981, pp.
　　　　10-14.
　　1982 "The effect of education on religious be-
　　　　lief." <u>Free Inquiry</u> 2: 26-31.
　　1985 "The effect of intelligence on religious
　　　　faith" <u>Free Inquiry</u> 5:

Bello, F.
　　1954 "The young scientists." <u>Fortune</u> 10 (June):
　　　　142-48.

Bender, I. E.
　　1968 "A longitudinal study of church attenders
　　　　and nonattenders." <u>JSSR</u> 7: 230:37.

Benson, J. M.
　　1981 "The Polls: A Rebirth of Religion?"
　　　　<u>Public Opinion Q</u>. 45: 576-85.

Berelson, B., and G. A. Steiner
　　1964 <u>Human Behavior</u>. New York: Harcourt, Brace,
　　　　& World.

Berger, P. L.
　　1969 <u>A Rumor of Angels</u>. Garden City: Doubleday

Boldt, W. M., and J. B. Stroud
　　1934 "Changes in the attitudes of college
　　　　students." <u>J. of Educa.</u> 25: 611-19.

Brown, D. G., and W. L. Love
　　1951 "Religious beliefs...of college students."
　　　　<u>J. of Social Psychol</u>. 33: 103-29.

Bryant, M.D.,
　　1958 <u>Patterns of Religious Thinking of Univer-
　　　　sity Students as Related to Intelligence</u>.
　　　　Unpublished Ph.D. Thesis, University of
　　　　Nebraska.

Bugelski, R., and O. P. Lester
    1940 "Changes in attitudes in college." J. of
        Social Psychol. 12: 319-32.

Caplovitz, D., and F. Sherrow
    1977 The Religious Dropouts. Beverly Hills:
        Sage Publications.

Caplow, T., and H. M. Bahr
    1979 "Half a century of change in adolescent
        attitudes." Public Opinion Q. 43:
        1-17.

Caplow, T., H. M. Bahr, B. A. Chadwick, et al
    1983 All Faithful People, Change and Continuity
        in Middletown's Religion. Minneapolis, Un.
        of Minnesota Press.

Carlson, H. B.
    1934 "Attitudes of undergraduate students."
        J. of Social Psychol. 5: 202-13.

Carman, H. J., and H. C. Syrett
    1958 History of the American People. 2 vols.,
        N.Y., Alfred A. Knopf.

Chambers, J. A.
    1964 "Creative scientists of today." Science
        145 (9-11-64): 1203-05
    1965 "Reply to Datta." Science 146 (1-1-65): 67.

Chandler, R.
    1972 Public Opinion: Changing Attitudes on Con-
        temporary Political and Social Issues. N.Y.,
        R. R. Bowker.

Condorcet
    1979 The Progress of the Human Mind. Westport,
        Conn.: Greenwood Press.

Corey, S. M.
    1936 "Attitude differences between college
        classes: a summary and criticism." J. of
        Educa. Psychol. 27: 321-30.

    1940 "Changes in the opinions of female students
        after one year at a university." J. of
        Social Psychol. 11:341-51.

Davis, J. A.
  1976 Studies of Social Change Since 1948. Vol.I,
       Chicago: National Opinion Research Center.

  1982 General Social Surveys, 1972-82. Chicago:
       NORC.

Dudycha, G. J.
  1934 "The beliefs of college students concerning
       evolution." J. of Ap. Psycho. 18: 85-96
  1950 "The religious beliefs of college freshmen
       in 1930 and 1949." Reli. Edu. 45: 165-9.

Duncan, O.D., M. Schuman, and B. Duncan
  1973 Social Change in a Metropolitan Community.
       Beverly Hills, CA: Sage Publications

Edwards, R. H., J. M. Artman, and G. M. Fisher
  1928 Undergraduates, N. Y., Doubleday & Co.

Feldman, K. A., and T. M. Newcomb
  1969 The Impact of College on Students. Vol. II,
       San Francisco: Jossey-Bass, Inc.

Field, M. D.
  1981 "Poll shows state favors teaching of
       evolution." San Francisco Chronicle,
       May 15, 1982, p. 9.

Ford, T. R.
  1960 "Status, residence, and fundamentalist
       religious beliefs in the southern Appala-
       chians." Social Forces 39: 41-49.

Fortune
  1948 "The Fortune Survey." Fortune 38 (Dec.):
       39-56.

Franzblau, A. N.
  1934 Religious Belief and Character among Jewish
       Adolescents. N.Y., Teachers' College
       Contributions to Education, No. 64.

Gaede, S.
  1977 "Religious Participation, socioeconomic
       status, and belief-orthodoxy." JSSR 16:
       245-53.

Gallup, George H. (Gallup Poll)
    1972 The Gallup Poll, Public Opinion 1935-71.
        N.Y. Random House.

    1976 "Religion in America." The Gallup Opinion
        Index, Report No. 130.

    1978 The Gallup Poll, Public Opinion, 1972-77.
        Vol. I & II., Wilmington, Del.: Scholarly
        Resources.

    1979 The Gallup Poll, Public Opinion, 1978.
        same publisher.

    1981 The Gallup Poll, Public Opinion, 1980. same
        publisher.

    1982a The Gallup Poll, Public Opinion, 1981. same
        publisher

    1982b "Religion in America, 1981-1982." The
        Gallup Report, June-July, 1982.

    1983a The Gallup Poll, Public Opinion, 1982.
        Wilmington, Del.: Scholarly Resources.

    1983b "Religion in America, 1983." The Gallup
        Report, No. 16, August, 1983.

Gallup, George, Jr.
    1982 "Life after death." McCall's Magazine, June,
        1982.

Garrison, K. C., and M. Mann
    1931 "A study of the opinions of college students."
        J. of Social Psychol. 2: 168-77.

Gilliland, A. R.
    1940 "The attitude of college students toward God
        and the church." J. of Social Psychol. 11:
        11-18.

    1953 "Changes in religious beliefs of college
        students." JSP 37: 113-16.

Glenn, N. D., and E. Gotard
    1977 "Religion of Blacks in the U.S." Am. J. of
        Sociol., 83: 443-51.

Glenn, N. D., and R. Hyland
    1967 "Religious preference and worldly success."
         Am. Sociol. R., 32: 73-85.

Glenn, N. D., and D. Weiner
    1969 "Some trends in the social origins of
         American sociologists." Am. Sociologist, 5:
         291-302.

Glock, C. Y., and R. Stack
    1965 Religion and Society in Tension. Chicago:
         Rand McNally & Co.

Goldsen, R. K., M. Rosenberg, R. M. Williams, and E. A.
    Suchman 1960 What College Students Think. N.Y.,
         D. Van Nostrand Co.

Gragg, D. B.
    1942 "Religious attitudes of denominational
         college students." J. of Social Psychol.
         15: 245-54.

Greeley, A. M.
    1970 "Influence of the religious factor." in
         Religion, Culture, and Society, edited by
         Louis Schneider.

Hadden, J. K.
    1963 "An analysis of some factors associated with
         religion and political affiliations in a
         college population." JSSR 2:2, 209-16.

    1969 The Gathering Storm in the Churches. N.Y.,
         Doubleday.

Harper, M. H.
    1927 Social Beliefs and Attitudes of American
         Educators. N.Y., Bureau of Publications,
         Teachers College, Columbia University.

Hastings, P. K., and D. R. Hoge
    1970 "Religious change among college students over
         two decades." Social Forces 49: 16-27.

    1976 "Changes in religion among college students."
         JSSR 15: 237-49.

Havens, J.
    1964 "A study of religious conflict in college
         students." J. of Social Psychol. 64: 77-87.

Heath, P. H.
1969 "Secularization and maturity of religious belief." J. of Relig. and Health 8: 335-58.

Hites, R. W.
1965 "Change in religious attitudes during four years of college." J. of Social Psychol. 66: 51-63.

Hoge, D. R.
1971 "College students value patterns in the 1950's and 1960's." Sociol. of Educa. 44: 170-97.

1974 Commitment on Campus. Philadelphia: Westminster Press.

Hoge, D R., and J. E. Dyble
1981 "The influence of assimilation on Protestant ministers' beliefs, 1928-78." J. for the Sci. Study of Religion 20: 64-77.

Hoge, D. R., and L. G. Keeter
1976 "Determinants of college teachers' religious beliefs." JSSR 15: 221-35.

Hollingshead, A.B.
1975 Elmtown's Youth and Elmtown Revisited. N.Y.: John Wiley & Sons.

Howells, T. H.
1928 "A comparative study of those who accept as against those who reject religious authority." U. of Iowa Studies in Character. Vol, 2, No.2.

Hunter, E. C.
1942 "Changes in general attitudes of women students during four years in college." J. of Social Psychol. 16: 243-57.

1951 "Attitudes of college freshmen: 1934-49." J. of Psychol. 31: 281-96.

Jones, E. S.
1926 "The opinions of college students." J. of App. Psychol. 10: 427-36.

Jones, V.
    1936 "Attitudes of college students towards war,
        race, and religion and the changes in such
        attitudes during four years in college."
        Psycho. Bul. 33: 731-32.
    1938 "Attitudes of college students" Part II,
        J. of Edu. Psychol. 29: 1, 114-34.

    1970 "Attitudes of college students and their
        changes: a 37-year study." Genetic Psychol.
        Mono. 81: 3-80.

Katz, Daniel, and F. H. Allport
    1931 Students' Attitudes. Syracuse, N.Y.:
        Craftsman Press.

Kelley, E. L., and D. W. Fiske
    1951 The Selection of Clinical Psychologists.
        Ann Arbor: U. of Michigan Press.

Kosa, J., and C. O. Schommer
    1961 "Religious participation, knowledge, and
        scholastic aptitude: an empirical study."
        JSSR 1: 88-97.

Kuhlen, R. G., and M. Arnold
    1944 "Age differences in religious beliefs and
        problems during adolescence." J. of Genetic
        Psychol. 65: 291-300.

Lehman, H. C., and P. A. Witty
    1931 "Scientific eminence and church membership."
        Scientific Monthly 33: 54-49.

Lehman, I. J.
    1963 "Changes in critical thinking, attitudes,
        and values from freshman to senior years."
        J. of Edu. Psychol. 54: 305-15.

Leuba, J. H.
    1934 "Religious beliefs of American Scientists."
        Harper's 169: 297-306.

    1950 The Reformation of the Churches. Boston:
        Beacon Press.

Lipset, M. L.
    1959 "Religion in America." Columbia U. Forum,
        Winter, 1959, pp. 17-21.

Marty, M. E., S. E. Rosenberg, and A. M. Greeley
    1968 What Do We Believe? The Stance of Religion
        in America. N.Y., Meredith Press.

Morison, S. E., H. S. Commager, and W. E. Leuchtenburg
    1980 The Growth of the American Republic, Vol.
        II, 7th ed. N.Y., Oxford Univ. Press.

National Review
    1971 "Opinion on the campus." National Review,
        June 15, 1971, pp. 635-50.

Nelson, E.
    1940 "Student Attitudes toward the reality of
        God." Genetic Psychol. Mono. 22: 373-423.

Niemi, R. G., R. D. Ross, and J. Alexander
    1978 "The similarity of political values of
        parents and college-age youth." Public
        Opinion Q. 42: 503-20.
Ostheimer, J. M., "Euthanasia." Pub. Op. Q. 44:123.
Parker, C. A.
    1971 Changes in religious beliefs of college
        students" in Research on Religious Develop-
        ment (1971), edited by M.P. Strommen. N.Y.,
        Hawthorn Books.

Perkins, D., and G. G. Van Deusen
    1968 The United States of America, A History.
        Vol. II, 2nd ed.

Plant, W. T., and E. W. Minium
    1967 "Differential personality development in
        young adults of markedly different aptitude
        levels." J. of Educa. Psychol. 58: 141-52.

Poythress, N. G.
    1975 "Literal, antiliteral, and mythological
        religous orientations." JSSR 14: 231-84.

Putney, S., and R. Middleton
    1961 "Dimensions and correlates of religious ideo-
        logies." Social Forces 39: 285-90.

Rankin, F. S.
    1938 The Religious Attitudes of College Students.
        Nashville: George Peabody College for
        Teachers (#206).

Remmers, H. H., and D. H. Radler
    1957 The American Teenager. N. Y., Bobbs-Merrill,
    Inc.

Rigney, D., R. Machalek, and J. P. Goodman
    1978 "Is secularization a discontinuous process?"
    JSSR 17: 4, 381-87.

Roe, Ann
    1953 The Making of a Scientist. N.Y., Dodd, Mead,
    & Co.

Roof, W. C.
    1978 Community and Commitment. N.Y.: Elsevier.

Ross, M. G.
    1950 Religious Beliefs of Youth. N.Y.: Associa-
    tion Press.

Rossman, P.
    1960 "Religious values at Harvard." Relig. Educa.
    55: 24-29

Sinclair, R. D.
    1928 "A comparative study of those who report the
    experience of the divine presence and those
    who do not." U. of Iowa Studies in Character
    2: 3.

Smith, Page
    1980 The Shaping of America. Vol. III., N.Y.:
    McGraw Hill.

Southern, M.L., and W. Plant
    1968 "Personality characteristics of very bright
    adults." J. of Social Psychol. 75: 119-26.

Stark, R.
    1963 "On the incompatability of religion and
    science...." JSSR 3: 3-20.

Steinberg, S.
    1974 The Academic Melting Pot. N.Y.: McGraw-Hill
    Book Co.

Symington, T. A.
    1935 Religious Liberals and Conservatives. N.Y.:
    Teachers College, Columbia Un.

Terman, L. W.
    1959 The Gifted Group at Mid-Life. Stanford Un. Press.

Thalheimer, F.
    1965 "Continuity and change in religiosity, a study of academicians." Pac. Sociol. R. 8: 101-08.

    1973 "Religiosity and secularization" Sociol. of Edu. 46: 183-202.

Toch, H. H., R. T. Anderson, J. A. Clark, and J. J. Mullin 1964 "Secularization" in college: An exploratory study." Religious Educa. 59: 490-501.

Trent, J. W.
    1967 Catholics in College. Chicago: Univ. of Chicago Press.

Vaughan, T. R., D. H. Smith, and G. Sjoberg
    1965 "The religious orientation of American natural scientists." Social Forces 44: 519-26.

Vinacke, W. E., J. Eindhoven, and J. Engle
    1949 "Religious attitudes of students at the University of Hawaii." J. of Psychol. 28: 161-79.

Warren, J. R., and P. A. Heist
    1960 "Personality attributes of gifted college students." Science 132 (Aug. 5): 330-37.

Webster, H.
    1958 "Changes in attitudes during college." J. of Edu. Psychol. 49: 109-17.

Webster, H., M. B. Freedman, and P.H. Heist
    1962 "Personality Changes in College Students." in The American College, ed. by N. Sandford. N.Y., John Wiley, Inc.

Wickenden, A. C.
    1932 "The effect of the college experience upon students' concepts of God." J. of Religion 12: 242-67.

Wiebe, K. F., and J. R. Fleck
    1980 "Personality correlates of intrinsic,
        extrinsic, and non-religious orientations."
        J. of Psychol. 105: 181-87.

Wuthnow, R.
    1976 "Recent patterns of secularization: a problem
        of generations?" Am. Sociol. R. 41: 850-61.

    1978 Experimentation in American Religion.
        Berkeley: Univ. of California Press.

Wuthnow, R., and C. Y. GLock
    1973 "Religious loyalty, defections, and experi-
        mentation among college youth." JSSR 12:
        157-80.

Young, R. K., D. S. Dustin, and W. H. Holtzman
    1966 "Change in attitude toward religion in a
        southern university." Psychol. Reports 18:
        39-46.

Zelan, J.
    1968 "Religious apostasy, higher education, and
        occupational choice." Sociol. of educa. 41:
        311-79.

INDEX OF NAMES

Alexander, J., 98
Allport, F.H., 7, 44
Allport, G.W., 12, 21, 52
Alston, J.P., 74
Ament, W.S., 101
American Council on
    Education, 19-20, 23,
    63, 98
Anderson, R.T., 59, 69
Argyle, M., 2, 31, 39, 61,
    77, 78, 79, 82-3, 85, 89
Arnold, M., 51, 53
Arsenian, S., 51, 64
Artman, J.M., 44
Bahr, H.M., 7, 37, 72
Bain, R., 44
Barrett, D.B., 29-30, 103,
    118
Baumer, F.L., 4
Beit-Hallahmi, B., 61
Bello, F., 103
Bender, I.E., 104
Benson, J.M., 40
Berelson, B., 105
Betts, G.H., 31
Boldt, W.M., 47
Brandeis Univ., 18
Bonhoeffer, D., 4
Bryant, M.D., 55, 90
Bryn Mawr College, 5-7, 16,
    113
Bugelski, R., 47
California, State of, 21
California, Univ. of
    (Berkeley), 14
Caplovitz, D., 18, 21, 62,
    69, 96
Caplow, I., 7, 37, 72
Carlson, H.B., 86, 87, 88
Carman, H.J., 3
Carnegie Foundation, 23, 63,
    68
Catholic Digest, 23, 70,
    123

Chambers, J.A., 103
Chadwick, B.A., 37, 72
Chandler, R., 61
Chave, E.J., 9, 11, 48, 50,
    51, 86, 88
Clark, J.A., 59
Condorcet, 109
Commager, H.S., 3
Converse College, 10, 50
Corey, S.M., 48, 64, 86
Cox, Harvey, 41
Dartmouth College, 15
Darwin, Chas., 3-4
Davis, J.A., 112
DeJong, 69
Demareth, 39
Denver, Univ. of, 15, 55
Dudycha, G.J., 8, 46
Duncan, G.D. and B., 27
Dustin, D.S., 17, 56, 91
Dyble, J.E., 31
Edwards, R.H., 44
Eindhoven, J., 54
Engle, J., 54
Feldman, K.A., 42, 60, 90
Field, M.D. 29, 75
Fisher, G.M., 44
Fleck, J.R., 94
Ford, T.R.
Fisk, D.W., 102
Fortune Magazine, 52
Franzblau, A.N., 86, 88
Freidman, M.B., 57
Gaede, S., 71
Gaffin, Ben, 23, 70
Gallup, George H. (Gallup
    Poll), 24-26, 29, 34, 35,
    37, 39, 41, 53, 62, 68,
    72, 76, 104, 105, 109,
    115, 116, 119, 120, 123,
    127
Gallup, George, Jr., 33, 74,
    104
Garrison, K.C., 45

Gillespie, J.M., 12, 52
Gilliland, A.R., 11, 50,
    55, 88
Glenn, N.D., 68, 71
Glock, C.Y., 14, 57, 60, 96
Goldsen, R.K., 95
Goodman, J.D., 39
Gragg, D.B., 51, 55, 63, 89
Greeley, A.M., 70, 97, 98
Hadden, J.K., 11, 32, 58,
    64, 91
Harder, L, 71
Harper, M.H., 47, 67
Harris Poll, 29
Harvard Univ., 12-13, 52,
    54
Hastings, P.K., 15, 53, 61,
    64, 93
Havens, J., 56
Haverford College, 14
Hawaii, Univ. of, 54
Heath, P.H., 13
Heist, P.H., 57, 99, 123
Hemlock Quarterly, 29
Hites, R.W., 59, 64
Hoge, D.R., 2, 6-16, 21,
    31, 36, 37, 53, 61, 65,
    69, 93, 119
Hollingshead, A.B., 36
Holtzman, W.H., 17, 56, 91
Horton, P.B., 54
Howells, T.H., 54-5, 86, 88,
    89
Hunt, R.A., 93
Hunter, E.C., 10, 21, 50,
    64
Hyland, R., 71
James, Wm, iii-iv,
Jones, E.S., 43
Jones, V., 9, 37, 44, 64,
    88
Katz, Daniel, 7, 37, 44
Kaufman, J.H., 71-72
Keeter, L.G., 65, 69

Kelley, E.L., 102
Kosa, J., 90
Kuhlen, R.G., 51, 53
Ladinsky, 69
Lehman, H.C., 102
Lehman, I.J., 58, 64
Lenski, G.E., 118
Lester, O.P., 47
Leuba, J.H., iii-iv, 4,
    5-8, 22, 37, 41, 43,
    53, 66, 101, 103, 119
Leuchtenberg, W.E., 3
Lipset, M.L., 38-39
Little, C.C. 101
Los Angeles City College,
    13, 16
Lowe, W.L., 55, 89
Lynd, R. and H., 7, 72
Machalek, R., 39
Man, M., 45
Marquette Univ., 18
Marty, M.E., 70
Michigan Univ. of, 15, 40
Middleton, R., 56
Middletown, 7, 72
Minium, E.W., 92
Morison, S.E., 3
Mourier, 4
National Review, 17-18, 21,
    96
National Opinion Research
    Center, 11, 18-19, 28,
    62, 112
Nelson, E., 48
Newcomb, T.M., 42, 90
Newsweek, 33, 109
Niemi, R.G., 98
Northwestern Univ., 11, 50
Ostheimer, J.M., 29
Ousely, Wm, 38
Parker, C.A., 42, 60, 90
Perkins, D., 3
Plant, W.T., 92, 100
Polling, D., 33

Poythress, N.G., 82-3, 93
Putney, S., 56
Radcliffe College, 12-13, 52
Radler, D.H., 53, 63
Rankin, F.S., iv, 49, 64
Remmers, H.H., 53, 63
Rigney, D., 39
Ripon College, 8, 47
Roe, Ann, 102
Roof, W.C., 72
Roper, E., 52
Rosenberg, M., 95
Ross, M.G., 54
Ross, R.D., 98
Rossman, P., 13, 37
San Francisco Chronicle, 33
Schuman, H., 17
Sinclair, R.D., 85, 88
Sheldon, W.H., 9
Sherrow, F., 18-19, 21, 62, 69, 96
Sjoberg, G., 104
Smith, D.H., 104
Southern, M.L., 100
Starbuck, E.D., iii-iv
Stark, R., 57, 96
Steinberg, S., 23, 30, 68, 69
Sternberg, R., 82
Stroud, J.B., 47
Steiner, G.A., 105
Symington, T.A., 47, 87
Syracuse,Univ., 7
Syrett, H.C., 3
Telford, C.W., 92
Terman, L.W., 86, 99
Texas, University of, 17
Thalheimer, F., 67
Thurstone, L.L., 9, 11, 48, 50, 51, 86-7.
Time (Magazine), 28, 30, 109
Toch, H.H., 59, 64
Trent, J.W., 59, 64, 92
Van Deusen, G.G., 3
Van Tuyl, M.C., 54
Vassar, 55
Vaughan, T.R., 104

Vinacke, W.E., 54
Warren, J.R., 99, 123
Weber, Max, 38
Webster, H., 55, 59, 64
Wickenden, A.C., 45
Wiebe, K.F., 94
Weiner, D., 68
Wilenski, 69
Williams College, 15,53
Wisconsin, Univ. of, 9, 11, 47
Witty, P.A., 102
Wuthnow, R., 14, 17, 21, 27-28, 60, 93, 113
Yankelovich, D., 61
Young, J., 12, 52
Young, R.K., 17,56, 91
Young, R.K., 91
Y.M.C.A., 54
Zelen, J., 11, 21, 96

143

ABOUT THE AUTHOR

Born in Carthage, Missouri, in 1904, and raised largely in Pasadena, California, Burnham Putnam Beckwith was graduated from Stanford University with an A.B. in philosophy in 1926. He spent the next two years at the Harvard Business School and, after three more years of full-time study, received a Ph.D. in economics from the University of Southern California in 1932. He held a postdoctoral research-training assistantship under Dr. Edward L. Thorndike at Teacher's College, Columbia University, from 1935 to 1937.

After a brief university teaching career, Dr. Beckwith was employed by various federal war agencies from 1941 to 1949. Since 1949 he has devoted his life to private research and writing. He has published a dozen books, including Ideas About the Future, A History of Futurism, 1794-1982, (1984); Radical Essays, On Social Policy, Religion, and Ethics (1981); Free Goods. The Theory of Free or Communist Distribution (1976); Government by Experts, The Next Stage in Political Evolution (1972); The Next 500 Years, Scientific Predictions of Major Social Trends (1967); and Religion, Philosophy, and Science, An Introduction to Logical Positivism (1957).